THEATRE ART

THEATRE ART

EDITED AND WITH AN INTRODUCTION BY

LEE SIMONSON

CONTRIBUTIONS BY

ALLARDYCE NICOLL   JOHN ANDERSON

PAUL ALFRED MERBACH   OLIVER M. SAYLER

JOHN MASON BROWN

COOPER SQUARE PUBLISHERS, INC.
NEW YORK
1969

Originally Published 1934
Published by Cooper Square Publishers, Inc.
59 Fourth Avenue, New York, N. Y. 10003
Standard Book Number 8154-0289-9
Library of Congress Catalog Card No. 74-79205

Printed in the United States of America

CONTENTS

Plates

THE EXHIBITION HAS BEEN SELECTED FROM THE FOLLOWING COLLECTIONS:

NICOLAI AKIMOFF, LENINGRAD

THE ESTATE OF ADOLPHE APPIA, GENEVA

WILLI BAHNER, VIENNA

ANDRÉ BARSACQ, PARIS

MRS. S. BASHKIROFF, NEW YORK

DR. ADOLPH BEHNE, BERLIN

MRS. ALINE BERNSTEIN, NEW YORK

MARTIN BIRNBAUM, NEW YORK

MRS. LESLEY BLANCH, LONDON

GEORGE BLUMENTHAL, NEW YORK

CLAUDE BRAGDON, NEW YORK

M. BRODSKY, LENINGRAD

KENNETH CLARK, OXFORD, ENGLAND

PAUL COLIN, PARIS

JACQUES DALCROZE, GENEVA

HEINZ DANIEL, HAMBURG

THE DUKE OF DEVONSHIRE, CHATSWORTH, BAKEWELL, ENGLAND

WALTER DEXEL, LONDON

HENRY DREYFUSS, NEW YORK

MANUEL ESSMAN, NEW YORK

J. KYRLE FLETCHER, LTD., NEWPORT, ENGLAND

MRS. LOVAT FRASER, LONDON

WALTER RENÉ FUERST, PARIS

MRS. JOHN W. GARRETT, BALTIMORE

NORMAN BEL GEDDES, NEW YORK

MISS LILLIAN GISH, NEW YORK

ROCHUS GLIESE, ESSEN

MORDECAI GORELIK, NEW YORK

DR. JOSEPH GREGOR, VIENNA

HEINZ GRETE, NUREMBERG

MR. R. HALL, TONBRIDGE WELLS, ENGLAND

MRS. ARTHUR HEATON, BIRMINGHAM, ENGLAND

HEINZ HELMBACH, MAGDEBURG, GERMANY

M. HEYTHUM, PRAGUE, CZECHOSLOVAKIA

VLASTISLAV HOFMAN, PRAGUE, CZECHOSLO-VAKIA

SIDNEY HOWARD, NEW YORK

WALTER HUSTON, HOLLYWOOD

MRS. EDITH ISAACS, NEW YORK

DR. SMITH ELY JELLIFFE, NEW YORK

ROBERT EDMOND JONES, HOLLYWOOD

JONEL JORGULESCO, NEW YORK

NAT KARSON, NEW YORK

VALENTIN KODOSEVITCH, LENINGRAD

MICHEL LARIONOFF, PARIS

ARCH LAUTERER, BENNINGTON, VERMONT

MOISEI LEVINE, LENINGRAD

EDOUARD LÖFFLER, MANNHEIM, GERMANY

LILLAH McCARTHY, O. B. E. (LADY KEEBLE), LONDON

MRS. E. C. MacVEAGH, NEW YORK

ADOLPH MAHNKE, DRESDEN

ROLF DE MARÉ, PARIS

LADISLAS MEDGYES, PARIS

OLIVER MESSEL, LONDON

JO MIELZINER, NEW YORK

MISS FANIA MINDELL, NEW YORK

TRAUGOTT MÜLLER, BERLIN

JAN MUNCIS, RIGA, LATVIA

DONALD M. OENSLAGER, NEW YORK

ROLLO PETERS, NEW YORK

EMIL PIRCHAN, PRAGUE, CZECHOSLOVAKIA

HANS POELZIG, BERLIN

JAMES REYNOLDS, NEW YORK

PAUL ROSENBERG, PARIS

CHARLES ROSNER, BUDAPEST

In addition to those who have lent to the exhibition the President and the Trustees of The Museum of Modern Art wish to thank the following:

For their generous contribution of special articles to the catalog:

MR. JOHN ANDERSON, NEW YORK

MR. JOHN MASON BROWN, NEW YORK

HERR PAUL ALFRED MERBACH, BERLIN

PROF. ALLARDYCE NICOLL, YALE UNIVERSITY

MR. OLIVER M. SAYLER, NEW YORK

For their assistance in assembling the exhibition:

MR. HARALD ANDRÉ, STOCKHOLM

DR. AGNE BEIJER, DIRECTOR, DROTTNING-HOLM THEATRE MUSEUM

M. HENRI BERNSTEIN, PARIS

MME. HENRI BERNSTEIN, PARIS

MR. MARTIN BIRNBAUM, NEW YORK

MR. PETER A. BOGDANOV, NEW YORK

MR. CHARLES B. COCHRAN, LONDON

M. ROLF DE MARÉ, PARIS

DR. W. DEONNA, DIRECTOR, MUSEUM OF ART AND HISTORY, GENEVA

MR. ASHLEY DUKES, LONDON

M. CHARLES DULIN, THÉÂTRE DE L'ATELIER, PARIS

MR. A. C. ENSOR, LONDON

DR. O. L. FOREL, GENEVA

DR. OTTO W. GARTHE, STUTTGART

M. LOUIS GIELLY, CURATOR, MUSEUM OF ART AND HISTORY, GENEVA

DR. JOSEPH GREGOR, VIENNA

GEHEIMRAT MAX GRUBE, MEININGEN

FRAU HEDWIG HAAG, STUTTGART

MRS. BLANCHE HAYS, PARIS

MR. OLOF H. LAMM, CONSUL GENERAL OF SWEDEN, STOCKHOLM

PROF. LILIE, CIVIC THEATRE MUSEUM, MEININGEN

DR. FRANZ RAPP, DIRECTOR, THEATRE MUSEUM, MUNICH

MME. M. SERT, PARIS

M. SIL-VARA, VIENNA

DR. BORIS SKVIRSKY, CHARGÉ D'AFFAIRES FOR THE U. S. S. R., WASHINGTON

THE SOCIETY FOR CULTURAL RELATIONS WITH FOREIGN COUNTRIES, MOSCOW

DR. FRANK TETAUER, MUNICIPAL THEATRE, PRAGUE

MR. FRANCIS THOMPSON, LIBRARIAN, CHATS-WORTH, DEVONSHIRE

PROF. KARL VON STOCKMAYER, COURT LIBRA-RY, STUTTGART

DR. ERIC WETTERGREN, DIRECTOR, STATE DRA-MATIC THEATRE, STOCKHOLM

MISS MARY HOYT WIBORG, NEW YORK

MR. NORMAN WILKINSON, LONDON

For their assistance in preparing the catalog:

PROF. HENRY WADSWORTH LONGFELLOW DANA, CAMBRIDGE

MISS HELEN FRANC, NEW YORK

MRS. EDITH ISAACS, NEW YORK

MRS. MILLARD MEISS, NEW YORK

MISS DOROTHY MILLER, NEW YORK

MR. DONALD M. OENSLAGER, NEW YORK

MR. OLIVER M. SAYLER, NEW YORK

MISS MARGARET SCOLARI, NEW YORK

MRS. LEE SIMONSON, NEW YORK

THE PRESIDENT AND TRUSTEES OF THE MUSEUM OF MODERN ART EXTEND TO

MR. LEE SIMONSON

THEIR GRATITUDE FOR THE GENEROUS CONTRIBUTION OF HIS SERVICES AS DIRECTOR OF THE EXHIBITION.

THE DESIGNER IN THE THEATRE

By Lee Simonson

I. ARTISTS AND ART-ARTISTS

The Hon. John R. Hylan, while mayor of New York, made a valuable contribution to the vocabulary of art criticism. He invented the term "art-artist." It has been too little used. The distinction between an art-artist and an artist is a real one, as I realized afresh while getting together the drawings and sketches for this exhibition of theatre art. An art-artist consciously produces a work of art that is wholly aesthetic in its appeal and is designed to arouse only a special sense, the aesthetic sense, which is a purification of our ordinary sensations of touch and sight. These are habitually impure because contaminated by associations and desires which have nothing to do with art, so that for centuries the majority of persons preferred to look at pictures of Madonnas rather than portraits of melons, just as in seeking for beauty in their environment they were inclined to contemplate mountains rather than mole hills. The immense labor of art criticism in the last fifty years has aimed to end this anomaly, to purify art and our experience of it. Art has been successfully divorced from use, beauty from subject matter, and the aesthetic emotion disentangled from the extraneous emotions that once created heroes, heavens and hells. The aesthetic sense is now cultivated by an arduous process of contemplation, of which a select number of connoisseurs and art critics is capable. They decide whether or not a painting or statue is sufficiently pure to be known as a work of art. The art-artist's statues on pedestals or pictures in gold frames, like children dressed for a party, usually have no place to go until they are invited to an exhibition where the judgment is made. The public is then invited in, so that it may learn to recognize a work of art after being told what a work of art is.

Unfortunately there is still no general agreement as to how pure pure art can be or exactly what form the purification is to take. Until recent years at least the professional critics proved extremely unreliable. They invariably ridiculed, damned or ignored the work of every aesthetic innovator, who was as a rule first recognized by poets or novelists such as Gautier, Huysmans, Zola, George Moore or Gertrude Stein, and was then widely acclaimed as an artist only after he had died in poverty like van Gogh, in obscurity like Cézanne, or was being trundled about in a wheel chair like Renoir in his old age. Even the innovators themselves often failed to recognize one another. Manet (according to Vollard) once remarked to Monet, "As a friend of Renoir you really ought to advise him to give up painting. You can see for yourself how little aptitude he has for it."

The purification of art is now so holy a cause that the fate of art is more important than the fate of the artist. As one English critic, Mr. Wilenski, has put it: "The first stage in art appreciation is to distinguish the work of a hack painter from that of a true artist. . . . It is always hard to distinguish contemporary *artists*. It is much easier to pick out the true artist of a period that is past. When an artist has been dead for thirty or fifty years we can see him in relation to his period and to the other artists who have worked before." Which perhaps helps to explain why during the last century so many geniuses among painters earned such princely livings only after they were dead. The great painter is accorded the privilege of martyrdom; we make sufficient amends by beatifying him thirty or fifty years too late. Our museums tend to become heavens where the pure artists are ranged in eternal hierarchies around the throne of Art, like saints seated in immutable tiers at the feet of God. Our exhibitions are dress rehearsals for a Last Judgment. And a work of art to-day, more than ever before, is either a sacred relic or a living mystery.

Before attempting to review the work in this exhibition, done for the theatre during three centuries by painters and architects, it is well to remind ourselves that even in their own day they were not art-artists, but artists, content to be necessary craftsmen, and rarely needed as an incentive the conviction that they were producing a work of art or contributing to the development of art history. Their work with few exceptions was ordered and paid for by actors and theatre managers because it could add to the glamour and the excitement of an actual performance in a theatre, and they, like the public that enjoyed and applauded a stage setting, were quite unconcerned as to whether or not the original sketch was worth preserving. Indeed, designs for stage settings were as unimportant to the public which created a demand for them as were the architects' plans for the cathedrals in which the same public worshiped, or as the shipwrights' models for the galleons that opened new horizons and brought back gold from the Indies. In this respect designs for the stage are not unlike many of the objects now classified as works of art in our museums, objects that could not have been collected while they were being produced without pulling chairs from under the worthies who were sitting on them, dismantling priests, violating tombs or desecrating altars. Designs for the theatre are impure art, now known derogatively in aesthetic circles as applied or decorative art, and are produced by much the same process which to-day gives us buildings or bridges that also express the taste, the temper, and the culture of an epoch. Like a bridge or a building they are so much a part of contemporary life that their aesthetic value cannot be wholly isolated in an exhibition hall; they have often been destroyed, lost or forgotten long before anyone realized that they might be important landmarks in the aesthetic development of a nation or a continent.

But so persuasive is our new-found concern for the purity of art that it is safeguarded even by our customs authorities, who recently decided that the material in this exhibition was not entitled to free entry, even temporarily, into this country. These drawings, in the eyes of the guardians of the Port of New York, cannot be considered as original works of art; they are merely an intermediate step in the production of something essentially commercial. And this ruling has been, on a previous occasion, sustained by a decision of the United States Supreme Court. Thus a painting which may have been sold and resold with mounting profits for successive owners and picture dealers can be brought into this country as a pure expression of beauty and appropriately hung in a museum. This is not a commercial enterprise but the disinterested process by which the pure in art is shunted to its ultimate shrine. The design for a stage setting, on the contrary, is tainted with commercialism from its inception and can safely be let in, like any other dubious character, only under bond.

But whether or not these drawings and sketches are art according to our modern definition of it, they are art in the antiquated sense of the term: they created a succession of pictorial conventions which made a reproduction of life more real than life itself. Like many works of art in periods less aesthetic than our own, they were part of an act of interpretation; their aesthetic values were determined by the art of the theatre of which they were a part, where they did enhance the grace and the gaiety, the glitter and the glamour, the terror and the sublimity of human experience. Many, even of the more recent designs, are the architecture of worlds we could no longer inhabit even if they were again embodied on the stage, the geography of lost kingdoms whose rulers we have deposed. Considered apart from their original rôle, as purely graphic art, these drawings can do no more than indicate their most expressive qualities that originally illustrated a vision of life which they helped to intensify. They are primarily working drawings. Even the drawings made for ideal rather than actual

13

stages are not self-sufficient but anticipations of an event: they are planned to make more significant the miming of life that is to take place within their projected confines.

This exhibition therefore is perhaps rather for the theatre-goer than for the aesthete. It may serve to revive our awareness of the variety and intensity of life as it has been lived in the theatre of yesterday and to-day. It may, by the record of unflagging fecundity of invention, reassure us that the designer in the theatre is occasionally creative, although necessarily so much less so than the creator who evolves a purely pictorial method of recording the importance of an apple, a tree or a naked woman. It may also serve as an augury that designers for the theatre of tomorrow will probably succeed in creating forms that can illustrate or symbolize the spectacle of human destiny as playwrights of the future conceive it.

II. CUPBOARDS AND PORTFOLIOS

Scenic designers to-day as in the past show a certain degree of indifference or contempt for the records of their productions. Many of the most important have been mislaid or lost. In an epoch when almost every other form of art is produced only to be exhibited, it was almost staggering to find artists completely indifferent to the need of exhibiting their work. Much of it I had to dig out of cupboards and old portfolios. It was difficult to get many of the designers to go to the expense of mounting these loose leaves. Framing in most cases was out of the question. Picasso told me he couldn't be bothered to look for the designs of "Le Tricorne." They were somewhere in his studio. But he couldn't take the time to find them. Besides he was very lazy. Derain refused categorically to send any of his ballet designs. They were too unimportant. As an art-artist he could be certain they were not art. Adolphe Appia's epoch-making designs are kept in a portfolio in the *Musée d'Art et d'Histoire* of his native city Geneva, in an annex to the library where they can be seen only on request. It has seemingly never occurred to the curators of that institution, who show tiled stoves, helmets and halberds, that these drawings are worthy of wall space as part of a permanent exhibit open to the public. Many of the designs of Inigo Jones, now among the treasures of the Duke of Devonshire's collection, are spattered with flakes of scene paint just as they originally came from some scene painter's work shop. Evidently they were also working drawings and not worth preserving carefully in their own day.

Only in the Soviet Union was it evident that contemporary stage settings were considered worthy material for a museum. Almost every theatre maintains its own museum, where models of its most important productions are preserved in chronological order. But there the difficulty was of another sort. Several of the more important theatre museums were closed preparatory to moving to new quarters.

I corresponded for three months before going abroad and traveled through half of Europe for two months. I should have corresponded for six months and stayed abroad a year. The exhibition is therefore incomplete. Many of the gaps have been filled by loans from private collections. Many remain. In the short space of time that I could stay abroad I was unable to arrange other loans with absentee owners, to trace many drawings, to get in touch with many artists and directors. Nevertheless the exhibition does give a fairly complete picture of the development of stage design from the 16th century to the present day. And it is possible to indicate on the basis of the examples displayed what the trend of that development has been.

III. DESIGNERS AND DOCTRINES

Scene painting, like painting of easel pictures in Europe, has evolved about an effort to enhance by reproduction our awareness of the third dimension. Painting in the Orient could remain flat without becoming insignificant. In the Occident painting could only become significant by perfecting methods of intensifying our sensations of plasticity, of three-dimensional form receding in space, ultimately filled with all the vibrations that refracted light could add to enveloping color. The sources of our aesthetic satisfaction are, as Bernhard Berenson defined them, tactile values and space composition. Most modern art criticism is based on his assertions originally made in 1896 in the *Florentine Painters*. "To realize form we must give tactile values to retinal sensations . . . the artist who gives us these values more rapidly than the object itself gives them, gives us the pleasures consequent upon a more vivid realization of the object. The chief business of the painter, as an artist, is to stimulate the tactile imagination. Unless it satisfies our tactile imagination, a picture will not exert the fascination of an over-heightened reality. . . . Space composition is not an arrangement to be judged as extending only laterally or vertically on a flat surface but extending inward in depth as well. Ordinary composition reduced to its elements, plays upon our feeling for pattern. Space composition is much more potent." Or as Clive Bell summarized the same convictions for the next generation when he exploited the phrase "significant form," "Pictures which would be insignificant if we saw them as flat patterns are profoundly moving because in fact we see them as related planes."

The fascination of over-heightened reality: to achieve this is also the dream of every worker in the theatre whether author, actor, director, or scene designer. But the centre of every dramatic presentation is already a living, three dimensional object—the actor. The designer's plastic problem therefore is a special one: to achieve an aesthetic unity between the actor and the world in which he moves. Since no stage is large enough to make the dimensions of this world absolute, the pictorial methods of illusion capable of stimulating our tactile imagination come into play.

The illusion with which pictorial stage setting began was the illusion of perspective. Its laws were rediscovered by the Renaissance as a result of the revival of interest in the classic theatre and the styles of classic architecture. Stage design was at first a by-product of architecture; the first text book of stage design is a chapter in Serlio's treatise on architecture published in 1537. The standard settings for tragedy and comedy are exercises in architecture, that by a combination of solid constructions such as columns, steps, obelisks, roofs, and overhanging cornices, together with painting in perspective, contrived to convey the spaciousness of a public square on a stage platform 17 feet in depth. Vasari's *Lives* contain descriptions of a number of contemporary settings more spacious and more elaborate, among them one that combined "a number of streets, palaces, temples, loggias and fanciful erections of all kinds . . . so perfectly represented that they did not look like things feigned . . . but entirely real and of noble extent." To create settings that seemed real and of noble extent was the ambition of the first Italian scene designers, who were echoed in England by Inigo Jones in his designs for Jonson's court masques and Davenant's operas. To the accepted architectural compositions of the day Inigo Jones added a typical English sensibility for landscape composition which the devices of perspective painting made possible. As a contemporary chronicler describes one setting: "the scenes behind seemed a vast sea from the . . . horizon of which was drawn by the lines of perspective, the whole work shooting downward from the eye; which decorum made it more conspicuous and caught the eye afar off with a wandering beauty . . . ."

Had the literary imagination of the Baroque been a classic one, its scenic designers might have achieved a formal architectural setting that seemed of noble extent and entirely real. But the literary imagination of the period promptly outgrew its classic models and became romantic, abandoning the classic unity of time and place for the kind of dramatic story that required incessant changes of scene. The need of quick scene-shifts prompted scenic artists to exploit the illusion of perspective painting and to abandon even an approximation of solid forms. The stage became a world of painted perspectives, framed in painted wings that converged towards a vanishing point on a painted backdrop, leading the eye to horizons that could catch the eye afar off with a wandering beauty. The delights of this symmetrical and balanced world, its stately distances and its towering heights, can be traced in the drawings of Berain, Vigarani, and the Bibienas, from the Drottningholm Theatre Museum. In the work of Despréz we can also trace the mounting romantic impulse particularly in landscape composition, the tendency to rely more and more on paint, less and less on even the semblance of architectural pattern, until in his later designs for the historical pageants of his royal patron, staged in the Drottningholm palace theatre at the end of the 18th century, he anticipated the methods that became traditional throughout Europe and remained unchallenged for nearly a hundred years.

By the middle of the 19th century one could not speak of scenic design but only of scene painting which degenerated into lifeless literalism. Many of Despréz' early settings are still preserved at Drottningholm. Like his sketches they are delicate in key, in tint a rosy grisaille or light sanguine with subtle gradations. A formal unity of tone is kept throughout. The total effect, particularly under the mellow candlelight of the period, emphasized by the converging lines of the architectural composition, maintains the illusion of form and space by the very delicacy of the painted indication. Fifty years later the prevailing academic palette with its dingy greens, murky browns, its rigid delineation of every detail and its leaden cast shadows, destroyed any illusion of atmospheric distance even on a backdrop. The increased illumination of the stage, due to the introduction of gas lighting, dissipated whatever illusion might have survived. Perspective scene painting became its own parody, a *trompe l'oeil* that no longer deceived the eye. George II, Duke of Saxe-Meiningen, felt obliged to issue instructions to the members of his court theatre company, warning them not to get too near the scenery; not to make gestures too violent lest they cause a house front to shake, not to lean on painted tree trunks or door posts for the same reason; not to stand too near a perspective backdrop where a hip might be on a level with a first story window or an elbow touch a chimney or a rooftop.

17

By 1870 this aristocratic amateur had completely revolutionized current methods of stage setting and become the father, or perhaps one should say the grandfather, of the so-called modern movement. He did this by making the actor the unit of his stage compositions, establishing as the basis of design the pattern of movement throughout a play. He developed the plasticity of his actors, particularly the movements of mobs and crowds, took Berlin by storm with a performance of Julius Caesar, repeated his triumphs on successive tournées in all the theatrical capitals of Europe, and profoundly influenced not only Antoine but Stanislavsky who was then about to start his Moscow Art Theatre. To the modern eye his settings are still literal and academic in many details, but they are nevertheless fundamentally architectonic, conceived not as painted pictures against which the actor moves, but spaces built about the actor in which and through which he moves, so that the general pattern of continued and interrelated movement, defined by surrounding planes and broken and varied stage levels, gives a continuous emotional force to any production. The Duke of Saxe-Meiningen's drawings were remarkable for their day because the actors are almost always indicated in them as an integral part of the stage composition, an essential part of the setting. The setting consists in the relation between the actors and their surroundings. An aesthetic unity was established by fundamentally relating the actor to the world in which he moved, which was no longer a picture of space but an arrangement of spaces that, in Berenson's words, stimulated the tactile imagination.

To Adolphe Appia this was merely preliminary. He conceived light itself as a plastic medium. His theories parallel in theatrical terms the discoveries of the impressionist and neo-impressionist painters as to the importance of vibrating light in establishing the tactile values of forms and projecting them in space. Paint and painted illusions had no place in Appia's theatre. Paint was nothing more than pigment to receive and reflect light. The color of the setting was the color of the light that filled it and was reflected from its surfaces, light that fluctuated subtly in endless gradations, keyed to the emotional pitch of the scene. A setting became a composition of forms related in space by the quality of the light that bound them together; its fluctuations, by the dramatic opposition of vast shadows and concentrated high lights, created monumental masses and then blotted them out until they were towering silhouettes or hung like mirages in the heavens. Berenson had written in 1896, "The direct effect of space composition is not only almost as powerful as that of music but is brought about in much the same way." In 1899 Appia wrote: "When stage pictures take on spatial forms dictated by music they are not arbitrary but have the quality of being inevitable." In Appia's drawings for Wagner's operas—among the most beautiful done for the modern theatre—stage setting achieves the direct emotional force and the fluidity of music.

They seem verifications of Pater's dictum "All art constantly aspires towards the condition of music." Yet they evoke a world that is not diaphanous or intangible, but as massive as the mountain tops, as vast as the starry spaces beyond them; here solid as stone and there palpitant as sunlight in a forest. The total effect is an illusion, for any form of stage setting, like every other effect in the theatre, is an illusion, but aesthetically it is a more perfect illusion, recreating so subtly and yet so monumentally in its pervading forms the world we live in. We are able to project ourselves into a stage equivalent which seems to move from "dawn to noon, from noon to dewy eve" and to heighten by its atmospheric mood the emotions that the actors are embodying in their persons.

The theories and the designs of Appia completely released the imagination of the modern stage designer. Most of my fellow critics however declare this was not accomplished until Gordon Craig published his more grandiose vistas, particularly the monolithic variations shown here, of which he wrote, "These etchings were made by the artist in the spring of 1907 and represent his most serious work. Connected as they are with his dream of an Ideal Theatre, they in no way have anything in common with the modern stage." "We must translate Movement through the medium of inanimate forms and there produce once more an Impersonal Art which shall take its place by the side of its two sister arts, Music and Architecture."

The modern theatre, nevertheless, in contrast to this Ideal Theatre, has remained personal, with the animate actor as its cornerstone. Most of the variations of modern stage design are variations of the perceptions of the Duke of Saxe-Meiningen and Adolphe Appia: the actor in motion as the basis of the total stage picture; the design, a space composition that can enhance the total pattern of movement and heighten its emotional intensity; light as a plastic element, binding the whole in a unity of mood. The influence of Appia's vision can be discerned in any number of recent productions, whether Reinhardt's "Dantons Tod" or Jessner's "Othello" and "Richard III," "The Tidings Brought to Mary," "Man and the Masses" or "Faust" at the Theatre Guild; in this exhibition in any number of designs, such as Robert Edmond Jones' drawings for

"Hamlet" and for "Green Pastures" where the light of hope beats upon the black faces and the massed brown robes; in Hofman's settings for the theatres of Prague, in Norman-Bel Geddes' projects for "King Lear" and the towering pinnacles for "La Divina Comedia."

But there have been counter currents—the impulse towards decoration and the impulse towards abstraction. The modern painter, with a revivified palette and a new-found technique of impressionistic suggestion of form, looked at a dingy stage and proceeded to enliven it. The Russian painter Golovin was among the first with his gleaming golden Kremlin for "Boris Godunoff," and eventually inspired the decorative debauch of the Ballets Russes. Fantasy of every kind has flowered flamboyantly everywhere in the theatre at one time or another in recent years; echoes and variations of almost every new school of painting, neo-impressionism, cubism, vorticism, futurism, expressionism, have found their way onto painted backdrops. But the theatre has also reflected the more formal preoccupation of cubism and abstract design in its stage architecture and simplified its stage structures. The third dimension has been stratified into the barest plinths and platforms, or reduced to the skeleton constructions that dominated the Soviet Theatre as recently as five or six years ago. Even then, like a skull, constructivism seemed to grin at its own death. The more recent Soviet designs, including those of its revolutionary theatres, when they are not frankly decorative, achieve a sober solidity which might be dubbed a new realism.

There has also been a tendency to deny altogether the necessity that the stage must suggest a world or create any illusion whatsoever, whether of three dimensional form, however abstract, or of composition in space. The stage, say these theorists, is always the stage, a performance is always a show. Let us be conscious of the fact, underline and outline the inherent artificiality of play acting and achieve a theatre frankly theatrical. The actor is a mime, his stage nothing more than a platform of one kind or another. The more clearly and nakedly we reveal it, the less illusion of any kind we strive for, the more effective will the performance be. The variations of these doctrines run all the way from Vakhtangoff's "Turandot," the designs for which I could unfortunately not procure, to the deliberate naiveté of Heythum's settings for "The Merchant of Venice" among others.

Theories multiply, doctrinaires cross swords and the theatre lives on. Which of its possible lives it may develop into a dominant method of production is perhaps indicated in this exhibition. If so I am unaware of it. I have selected none of this material to prove a theory, to indicate an aesthetic trend or to vindicate any school. I have borrowed wherever I could the work of men who were the acknowledged leaders of their native theatres and who impressed it with their imagination. And the artistic imagination in the theatre, like the artistic imagination everywhere in the modern world, is brilliant, at times overpowering, but short winded, veering incessantly under the winds of doctrine; is given to grandiose hopes, to violent experiments and equally violent reactions, unsustained as it is by a unified vision of man and society.

But the theatre that has died so many deaths continues to live many lives. This exhibition is a partial record of that vital and varied life, an echo of the intensity of life that we can vicariously achieve in the theatre, when we shuffle off the coil of our own egos, purge ourselves with laughter or with tears, grow wiser or wittier than we are, know love, pity and terror, dream and desire triumphantly. Such emotions are, alas, not wholly aesthetic and are undoubtedly impure. But the technique of achieving that emotional release is the art of the theatre. The design of a stage setting is an integral part of that art, and for that reason, if for no other, perhaps worth being recorded and remembered.

THE MASQUE DESIGNS OF INIGO JONES

By Allardyce Nicoll

In the year 1633 William Prynne, most resolute and uncompromising of Puritans, published an enormous quarto volume of more than a thousand pages (double column) entitled *Histriomastix*. In this he declared categorically that all plays were inspired by the devil, that all theatres were temples of sin, that one of the really popular amusements of Hell was a series of dramatic performances, and, in particular, that every actress was a "notorious whore." This last judgment got him, and others, into serious trouble. Certainly his statement, unqualified and unadorned, was an injudicious one when, but a few months previously, Queen Henrietta Maria had been taking part in plays and masques at court. Queens do not like being called such names; and we need not wonder that the worthy Prynne was haled before the Star Chamber, there to be sentenced to lose his ears. Earless he was set in the pillory, but in his loss he was destined to become a popular martyr. One more piece of fuel had been added by the Queen and by her King, Charles I, to that smouldering heap which was soon to blaze forth in general revolt. Charles I lost his head in causing Prynne to lose his ears.

The Puritan attack on the stage was largely due to the facts that the theatre generally had become, by the year 1633, a toy of the aristocracy and that royalty spent vast sums of public money in amusing itself with court masques. Richly glorious these masques must have been, the jewels glittering in the myriad candle lights and the rich silks shimmering as queens and princes and lords recited their lyric words or stepped gravely on the floor to dance. At best, however, they were but ephemeral things intended to be the vehicle for courtly acting in moments of diversion, and being so, their real splendour has utterly vanished. Only in two ways has something of them been preserved. In the printed texts composed by Ben Jonson, Sir William D'Avenant and others, we get the words that were spoken; while, more importantly, in the wonderful series of designs executed by Inigo Jones we have at least the basis on which was reared the magnificent stage spectacle of the seventeenth century. Six of these designs (preserved at Chatsworth, the home of the Duke of Devonshire) have been secured for the exhibition at the Museum of Modern Art.

Manifold is their interest. That they possess an intrinsic value of their own

22

will be obvious to all who visit the exhibition; but Jones was not merely an artist—he was as well a keen stage craftsman. He borrowed, certainly, from the flourishing theatres of Italy, but in borrowing he always added, giving to what he copied the grace of an individual touch. Through his inventive genius the masque in England became more than a mere replica of Italian Opera and Intermezzi. He tried out various ways of shifting scenery; independently of others he evolved that framework which later became the proscenium arch. Had he not been there to guide and inspire, the masque in England might have assumed a more literary development. As it was, Inigo Jones so imposed his personality upon the form that Ben Jonson, who had at the beginning given due credit to his scenic collaborator, growled out contemptuously that "painting and carpentry are the soul of masque," withdrew himself into his own study-shell, and, like a school-boy who will not play, moped and sulked.

Here at the very beginning of stage spectacle (for of that the Elizabethan playhouse was almost wholly innocent) is the age-long quarrel between the dramatist and the scenic artist—at least between the scenic artist and the dramatist who refuses to play the game. Jonson was surly, proud of his literary skill, suspicious of all that was not poetry. Shakespeare, greater than he, knew better. When the masque splendour in the reign of King James first came to dazzle men's eyes, Shakespeare, with his keen sense of theatric value, immediately seized on it and made it serve his own purposes. *The Winter's Tale* introduces its masque of shepherds; *Cymbeline* has its masque-like vision; and in *The Tempest* it is a masque of airy spirits that provides the occasion for one of the loveliest speeches ever written for actor to interpret:

> "And, like the baseless fabric of this vision,
> The cloud-capp'd towers, the gorgeous palaces,
> The solemn temples, the great globe itself,
> Yea, all which it inherits, shall dissolve,
> And, like this insubstantial pageant faded,
> Leave not a rack behind.   We are such stuff
> As dreams are made on, and our little life
> Is rounded with a sleep."

Though Inigo Jones' theatrically solemn temples and gorgeous palaces, raised in Whitehall to gladden the eyes of ladies and their lords, have faded like a dream, one wrack of time is left in these designs. The actual scenery, built at enormous cost, has perished, and the jewels worn by the actors (one lady is said to have had half a million's worth of gems on her person) no longer glitter on the lovely costumes. But in Inigo Jones' sketches we can get at least a faint vision of what once had been. Here is Oberon's fairy palace, first concealed in rocks and then opened to reveal delicate pillars and fantastically flimsy gateways; a moonlit landscape is put before us in one, in another a wealth of architectural detail such as was beloved in the seventeenth century, and in still another "a horrid Hell, the further part terminating in a flaming precipice, and the nearer parts expressing the Suburbs." On some of the Chatsworth sketches splashes of scene-painters' distemper still remain, for these were the actual designs used in the execution of the scenery. We may admire them for their beauty of line alone, but, in addition to that, those who are interested in the theatre may view these sketches with increased interest in that through them we are permitted to enter backstage of the royal playhouse at Whitehall, where for the first time painted scenery was adequately displayed before an English audience.

THE DROTTNINGHOLM THEATRE—
LOST AND FOUND*

By John Anderson

Some special glamour, which has no connection with aesthetic values, surrounds those waifs among works of art that have been lost and found again. It is as if Fate had changed its mind, and the public had been made privy to high transactions of the gods, so when mislaid treasures come to light they are enhanced by their one-time nearness to oblivion.

This is true of some seventy drawings in this exhibition, though that is, of course, not the reason why they are here. They were brought from the Drottningholm Theatre Museum because they are unique, and because no international exhibition of Theatre Art would be complete without them.

But in a more special way they are here for reasons beyond these of immediate interest, since they are really here because an inquisitive and sagacious scholar set out from the library in Stockholm one day in 1920 to hunt for a portrait he had heard was stored away in a cluttered old lumber room in the Winter Palace at Drottningholm. Fortunately for the world Dr. Agne Beijer knew treasure when he saw it. The lumber room turned out to be a forgotten Eighteenth Century Theatre, and its litter a collection of scenery and drawings that has become, under his wise curatorship, one of the sights of Europe. His cautious restoration has given to the whole place a special and lasting fascination which these drawings here reflect.

For in the genial enigmas of time and place that confront every traveller it is curious and paradoxical that a playhouse dedicated to illusion should evoke so powerful a sense of past reality as this Drottningholm theatre evokes of the Eighteenth Century. Even the most casual and insensitive visitor must feel in its auditorium the sentience of other times, that compelling quality of living that eludes even the acute evidence of more historic places. Lorenzo's seat amidst Gozzoli's chapel frescoes furnishes no Renaissance ghost for subtle understanding, any more than Napoleon's throne room does, or the countless scenes strewn over the world, once animated by breathing greatness. They are dead in time;

---

* Acknowledgment and thanks are accorded Mr. Albert Boni for permission to use in this article some material which has appeared in *Creative Art*.

25

preserved like mummies of lost illusion. We may be touched by them, for many different reasons, with a vague nostalgia, but they never live for us. At Drott-ningholm only a threshold offers easy barrier across a hundred and fifty years.

Something of this has to do, no doubt, with the inscrutable nature of theatres. Deserted, they lay upon the spectator a spell of their own, a hint of fundamental make-believe to which they stand, even empty, for silent witness. On the Queen's Island, outside of Stockholm, this little theatre does more than that, for it clings tenaciously to its own century, preserved in a sort of temporal vacuum. It is unique because it is physically intact. Its wooden machinery is as useful as it ever was. Its thirty settings have Eighteenth Century illusion in them because they were built for that illusion. They exist, so it exists, and its rows of benches for a vanished court present no greater denial of life than the empty benches of any modern theatre. A spectator is all that is needed to bring it to life and a spectator naturally steps across the threshold.

Essentially this is due to an accident of dynasty. When the Bernadottes took the throne of Sweden they preferred not to use this palace; so in the early part of the Nineteenth Century this theatre, which was built in 1764 for the sister of Frederick the Great and which still carries her initials in the fresh colors of its curtain, was forgotten in one of those happy lapses of memory to which even nations are subject. Wherefore the royal toy of Gustavus III, whose predilec-tions have recently subjected his ardours to modern psychoanalysis (with no small discredit), was forgotten along with its scenery, its stage designs, its costumes, and all the affectionate paraphernalia of a monarch who boasted, modestly enough for a monarch, that his was one of the two imaginations in Sweden. Desprez rejoiced in the other, and Desprez was the sponsor at Drottningholm of its obvious French influence.

Thus the playhouse remained for more than a hundred years a storeroom for royal rubbish, until the presiding dieties of art relented and sent Dr. Beijer on that wayward errand which was to produce such unexpected results. When he realized what he had found he clung to it with admirable obstinacy, cajoled money for restoration and support from astonishingly reluctant officials, and now presides serenely and affectionately over its assured destiny.

The wooden benches, which he found in a century's jumble, have been sorted and arranged according to the rank of their former occupants. Each has its origi-nal label, showing the social position of those entitled to sit on it. The rows rise in a gentle incline from the royal enclosure to the back wall, marked with the privileged tickets of those forgotten attendants, from cavaliers to ladies-in-waiting near the front, to the palace servants in the rear, and including, midway, such picturesque entitlements as "Keeper of the King's Great Watch" and "Palace Barbers." One bench alone raised a point of precedence, a row reserved for "Ladies Not Yet Presented to the King." A more liberal modern arbiter has put them nearer, perhaps, than Gustavus himself, with those same troublesome predilections, might have wished. Critics, obviously, were not necessary in a regal world of so many dilettantes.

These benches, of some three hundred places, fill the long and narrow auditorium, with two spaces where curtains could be drawn to shut off parts of the audience. One curtain could be closed immediately behind the royal enclosure for most private censorship; a second could shut out the palace servants from their paternal, but cautious, guardians.

The auditorium, with its Corinthian pilasters at the proscenium, blends perfectly into the stage so that players and playgoers seem to occupy one room —prophetic of later stagecraft. Six boxes depend from the side walls for use of the royal family, when it preferred to see without being seen. Two of the boxes have latticed grills to make them virtually impenetrable to unwanted observers.

But the stage itself is a mechanical marvel of strange survival. Even among modern stages it is enormous, designed for the production of opera, and it has a depth of nearly sixty feet. It rises steeply so that when an actor was upstage he was, in the original and literal sense, up. Its candle footlights, made from moulds preserved in the theatre's museum, could be dropped below stage level, and other candles, mounted on the wings in brackets that can still be worked on chains, shed upon the ancient sets a gentle glow that is suggested, more safely now out of respect for the antique, by small electric candles.

Old thunder machines are still workable, reminiscent of a forgotten inventor who, resenting the duplication of his device by a thieving manager, coined the reverberant but literal phrase that he was "stealing his thunder." Papier mâché waves, turning upon eccentric drums, suggest accurately the heaving urgency of the sea. The gods came down from heaven on jovial clouds, a trifle solid nowadays, perhaps, but duly and impressively Olympian, and devils popped up (with the assistance of sweating stage hands below at a back-breaking windlass) from infernos that must have seemed dark enough in those innocent times.

Furnishings, stoves, pianos, and even actors (perhaps the best of them) were painted charmingly and quite efficiently upon the canvas backdrops, making up

27

that Eighteenth Century world of illusion that is potent now because it brings us not only to its place but to its time, and helps us to peer with our own eyes through the key-hole of ancient make-believe into a lost world of graceful reality.

MODERN GERMAN THEATRE ART

By Paul Alfred Merbach*

The stage setting is a reflection of a period; it combines architectural, landscape, and figure elements. Its artistic evolution possesses a significance over and above its application in the theatre for it represents an illuminating cross-section of the history of art as a whole. In the forms and methods known to us to-day it is some three hundred years old. The forms of the baroque, rococo, classicism and naturalism can be seen outlined in its development as a sort of abbreviated chronicle. Galli-Bibiena and Karl Friedrich Schinkel, Quaglio's generation and the masters of Fritz Erler's school (ca. 1900) all shaped the theatre sense of their time. One made use of rustling splendor because the theatre, to him and to his age, was intensified, festive life and being; other designers employed austere lines expressing simplicity and greatness. Some paid a painfully accurate attention to historical truth, seeking to do justice even to stylistic details. Others again deliberately emphasized the bare essentials to make the stage setting truly serve the play. Splendor, austerity, authenticity and economy were consecutive dominants in scenic design. But in the second quarter of the Twentieth Century the theatre lays claim to the right of staging the theatre work of art, no matter what its period or its locale, in a manner determined solely by the thinking and emotions of *our* times. This means breaking with many a beloved tradition; but an age that seeks new forms and content of life is always compelled to blaze its own path.

Only in the distant future is any sort of goal to be discerned. There are, however, contemporary forces with a rightful claim to our attention. These forces can be reduced to the formula, perhaps, of transforming passive impressions into active expressions. We no longer want so much to delineate a form, as to evoke its meaning; not an image of the original, but as close an approach to the prototype itself, as is possible with the limited means available to human kind. The grandiose fiction, the gigantic As If, which the theatre has been and is, thus attains an even more powerful content, since the execution of such an aim can only consist in presenting symbols in place of superficial realities. This holds true beyond a doubt both for the spoken *and* sung theatre piece. This trend has

---

* Herr Merbach assembled the German section of this exhibition.

been aided—at least in Germany during the last few years—by numerous economic necessities everywhere affecting the complicated and costly operation of the theatre. The need for saving had to be harmonized with the necessity for giving the theatre its due: the adequate presentation of the play. Thus do ideal and practical demands of the day meet! It is untrue that in doing this a virtue is being made of necessity. Luckily enough, the creative will, arising out of the age, harmonizes with ineluctable influences of an external nature.

Adolphe Appia, the most important of whose settings are shown in this exhibition in authentic models, sought to follow this symbolic path more than thirty years ago in staging Richard Wagner's music dramas. Wagner's scenic visions stemmed from a period in which the German historical painters Piloty and Makart determined the forms prescribed for heroic events. They had a considerable influence upon the historical naturalism of the Meiningen school, as the examples exhibited here demonstrate. Appia, however, deviating from the traditional Wagner cult, began to create the settings for these music dramas "out of the music's spirit," that is he transferred the monumental lines of the interwoven motifs of the music to the stage setting, thus underscoring this symbolic music, "interpreting" it, and really completing Wagner's "total work of art." Adolphe Appia (died 1928) therefore became a pioneer and a stimulating force for the scenic design of to-day. His John the Baptist fate did not allow him to achieve final fulfillment, as it was only in very rare cases that he was able to put his creative ideas into actual settings.

Fritz Erler, whom we mentioned above, developed the "style theatre" around 1910 in the Munich Künstlertheater, in conformity with the limited space available on that stage. He let the dramatic flow play in a wholly neutral framework, or he used only what was absolutely necessary to project a "stylized" atmosphere. This was the road to expression, from Impressionism to Expressionism— but at the end of this road there stood the symbol. This is illustrated in two examples which cannot be shown in this exhibition. They deal with the cathedral scene in Goethe's "Faust," Part 1. In this scene the style theatre endeavored to convey the impression of a church or a chapel with suggestive means. It therefore offered an adumbration of the reality; not a nave with towering pillars that are lost in a twilight darkness, but a single column with a picture of the Virgin. An Expressionist stage setting, which seeks a single "expression" and raises it into a symbol, created (as in the design of Ludwig Sievert in Frankfurt-am-Main), a gigantic cross, filling the otherwise empty stage and even bursting

30

it apart as it leaned forward slightly. It is the symbol of all suffering and of all salvation. Gretchen, as the personified misery of mankind, crouches in all her futility and annihilation at the foot of the cross; the sinful, guilty individual almost disappears under the crushing weight of the burden upon her—and yet she is to become a guide to ethical-spiritual salvation.

Hans Sturm, who did stage settings in the former Düsseldorf Schauspielhaus under the direction of the late Luise Dumont, expressed a tragic-festive flow of events in the last act of Hebbel's "Herodes and Marianne," a tragedy of two congenial persons unable to understand each other, by eight or ten large illuminated cubes, using nothing but an empty space, on different levels, as the "arena" for the actors. This same designer employed a symbol of the Alps—a spiral drawn in a giant arc and interrupted by steps—for Byron's "Manfred" and his spiritual path along the heights. In Sturm's work we thus see the same creative will at work upon the play.

When Leopold Jessner began his highly original stage designs in the Berlin State Theatre some fourteen years ago, he discovered the now much-abused stairway as a poetic symbol. It was the conquest of a third dimension on the stage: height as well as breadth and recession. Now the whole effect could be intensified by elevating the actors. On the other hand, the steps made possible the achievement of a hitherto unattained differentiation of all scenic forces. A relationship of dependence, for instance, could now be given an illuminating and penetrating effect, by placing the persons involved on different steps. Scenic events of many types were thus accentuated.

The same urge and the same goal hold good for the opera of our day. Appia's endeavors pointed the way; here and there, it is true, he went too far in his otherwise altogether justifiable desire to avoid all that was superfluous. When he proposed to eliminate even the swan in a stage setting for Wagner's "Lohengrin," he affected the inner "romantic" life of the action, cutting it to the heart. On the other hand, the austere lines and the scenic design and continuity of the "Bauhaus" staging of "Fidelio" (State Opera House, Platz der Republik, Berlin, November 1927) by the late Ewald Dülberg, who died only a few months ago, represent a happy solution of a typical "salvation" opera, whose uninterrupted continuity of action requires the greatest tension.

The stage settings of topical operas, such as Krenek's "Jonny Spielt Auf," work with scenic methods which symbolically express only the barest essentials tangibly, leaving it to the audience to obtain the intended impression. This path

31

is quite usable for the heroic music drama as well, as was shown, for example, by the productions of Wagner with settings by Johannes Schröder (in Bochum and Duisburg in 1927). It was evident in a Lohengrin production (in Darmstadt 1929) staged by Schenk von Trapp. In this opera the castle courtyard of the second act all too often becomes the more or less successful imitation of a historical reality. In Darmstadt this solution was consciously avoided by creating a wall broken up by many windows, one of the men-at-arms appearing in each window. This yielded a stage setting that broke with all tradition, without losing appropriate dramatic effectiveness.

Thus, much that is new in scenic design is under way.

RUSSIA

THE DESIGNER AS COLLABORATOR

By Oliver M. Sayler

"They order these things better on the Russian stage."

Is that too familiar a refrain? Well, if it is, I cannot help it. I hardly thought myself, after fifteen years of service as interpreter of the Russian theatre to the western world, that I should ever again find a new case justifying this verdict. But I have. And the fact that I have is almost as exciting to me as the specific terms of the verdict. It is one more proof of the astonishing vitality of the Russian theatre.

This thing I've suddenly become aware they order better in Russia is the relationship of the designer to the producer on the stages of Moscow and Leningrad. As nowhere else in the world, the Russian stage designer is a true collaborator in the art of the theatre. As a corollary to that fact, here is another: Nowhere else have the greatest contemporary painters rallied so freely to the challenge and the opportunity of the theatre.

These conclusions may have been self-evident to others, and they must have been latent in my own consciousness, but I hit upon them quite unexpectedly in the course of trying to rationalize for myself the idea of an exhibition of the art of the theatre devoted primarily if not exclusively to stage design—to stage settings, stage costumes, stage lighting. This visible and physical sector of the composite art of the theatre is only one of four partners, the others being the playwright, the actor and the producer. You can't very well exhibit the contributions of these other partners—except in action on the stage of a theatre. An exhibition of the work of the stage designer, therefore, demands some statement of his relationship to these partners, especially to the one whom we call the producer, if it is to be something more than a stage designer's holiday, a glorification of one phase of the art of the theatre.

Relationship? That's what started the questions—and educed the verdict. Just where, I asked myself, does the stage designer come in, as they order things in Russia? The relationship must be very nearly perfect to be so unobtrusive as to escape my conscious attention all these years. I journeyed back in my memories and records.

33

Yes, there at the very birth of the Moscow Art Theatre, thirty-five years ago, were the celebrated contemporary painters, Victor Simoff and Nikolai Krimoff and Mstislaff Dobuzhinsky, providing backgrounds in the mood of spiritualized realism for the productions of Stanislavsky and Nemirovitch-Dantchenko, just as if they had always been integral parts of a perfect partnership. I doubt whether dramatic history will ever show a more extraordinary instantaneous collaboration of independent talents: directors, playwrights, actors—and scene designers.

Then and there began a practice which has followed down the years of the modern Russian theatre: In Russia, stage design is not—is never—a thing in itself; it is always the visual embodiment of a *theory* of the theatre. In Russia, stage design did not get out of hand; and, for that reason, it has never provided an argument, as it once did in this country, for conservative opponents of the modern theatre to denounce the whole movement as a stage designer's barbecue. Furthermore, since there were always producers, proceeding on the lines of clear-cut theories of the art of the theatre, Russian stage designers never had to become producers on their own account in order to create opportunities for self-expression, as they have occasionally been tempted to do in America, usually with disastrous consequences. Russian producers, fortunately, have always provided a constant challenge to Russian stage designers.

This is neither the place nor the time to analyze the various and varied theories of the theatre which have come and gone or stayed on the Russian stage in the last third of a century. It will be sufficient to name the outstanding theories and the producers most closely associated with them, and to cite the artists who collaborated with them in providing the desired scenic backgrounds.

The first major revolt against the spiritualized realism of the Moscow Art Theatre was led by Vsevolod Meyerhold who withdrew from the protection of the Sea Gull* to found his own Studio Theatre and later, in St. Petersburg, to reach his first great pinnacle as producer for Vera Kommissarzhevskaya. "The theatre theatrical," he called it; "stylization" is the more prevalent term. And to visualize this highly stylized revolt against realism he called on the services of such leading contemporary painters of the "Mir Iskusstva" and other secessionist groups as Anisfeld, Bondy, Sudeykin, Kulbin, Shervashidze, Korovin, Sapunoff, Bilibin, Denisoff and Dobuzhinsky, finally settling down to almost exclusive partnership with Alexander Golovin.

---

* Emblem of the Moscow Art Theatre.

34

Meanwhile, in western Europe, but soundly Russian for all that, Michel Fokine under the phoenix-wings of Diaghileff was calling to similarly sympathetic cooperation in caparisoning the lavish romanticism of the Russian Ballet such painters as Benois, Bakst, Roerich, Golovin, Korovin, and Anisfeld.

In due course, cubism, futurism, pro-unism, expressionism and even suprematism swept up into Russia from Europe or spontaneously sprouted in Moscow or St. Petersburg, turning the radicals of "Mir Iskusstva" into conservatives without the bother of moving a millimeter. But the new left wing painters were not left long without a theatre of their own, for Alexander Tairoff was at hand with his Kamerny Theatre, founded on a comparable dramatic theory, and destined to be the congenial stage home of Alexandra Exter, preceptress of our Boris Aronson; of Sudeykin, of Kuznetsoff, Larionoff, Gontcharova, Kalmuikoff, Lyentuloff, Miganadzhian, Yakuloff, Vyesnin, Stenberg and Ruindin.

A somewhat germane movement on the lyric stage, carrying expressionism into the hidebound opera, was the Musical Studio of Nemirovitch-Dantchenko which reached its height in the productions of "Carmencita and the Soldier" and "Lysistrata," familiar to American audiences, and particularly in the architecturally expressionistic settings of Rabinovitch.

The latest phase, constructivism, remains to be considered. First formally championed by Meyerhold in one of those startling *volte-face* which have characterized his career, this cross between the pictorial and the architectural, practically eliminating the former at times and paring the latter down to its skeleton, was foretold in certain early productions at the Kamerny and is the occasional credo to-day of the Vakhtangoff Theatre and Akhmetelli's Georgian National theatre, as well as of Meyerhold. In the nature of the case, the designer for the constructivist theatre is a stage carpenter and engineer rather than a painter, and it is for this reason that fewer names of general artistic significance appear in the records of these stages than formerly. Akimoff, Stepanova, Dmitrieff and their fellows are not and probably never will be easel or mural painters. Even as far back as Rabinovitch and "Carmencita," the stage designer as a highly specialized creative artist had made his appearance. In any record or analysis of the Russian theatre of the past decade, it is impossible to ignore this new kind of stage designer whose art begins and ends within the theatre. Whether or not he is a painter in the conventional sense, his relationship to the producer is on the same cooperative plane of mutual confidence, mutual respect and mutual enthusiasm with the producer.

For a time, during the days of compulsory propaganda in the Russian theatre
—roughly from 1925 to 1932—certain prophets predicted the displacement of
all other theories of the theatre by that of constructivism, since this bold, direct
and dynamic form of dramatic expression seemed best suited to the use of the
theatre as a political forum. With the unconditional return of the theatre to the
artists during the past year, however, the older traditional theories of the theatre have regained their former prestige, and, with them, the traditional artists
have again come into their own alongside the engineers of constructivism. They
never did wholly disappear, but it is particularly significant to realize that the
Moscow Art Theatre for its recent incomparable production of Gogol's "Dead
Souls" chose as its scenic artist the same Victor Simoff who had designed the
settings for "Tsar Fyodor Ivanovitch" and the first plays of Tchekhoff away
back in 1898.

It is significant to note, too, that in spite of the dislocations of Revolution and
the finally futile drafting of the theatre for direct political purposes, the same
main underlying theories of theatre have cut clean across revolutionary lines and
have persisted unbroken through social upheaval, taking color from the successive phases of that upheaval only as it is natural for the theatre to reflect the
topics and the points of view of its day. And, just as theory has persisted, so has
the practice of close and mutually stimulating cooperation between producer and
designer, to the end that the Russian stage designer still holds to-day a position
unique on the stages of the world.

THE AMERICAN THEATRE AND ITS DESIGNERS

By John Mason Brown

More than a hundred years ago, a general's son with a forehead like a bay-window and plenty of new ideas with which to fill it, wrote a brief prose preface that was taken as seriously by the budding Romantics of Paris as if it had been a sequel to the Book of Revelations. In the course of this inflammatory tract, he chanced to observe that "the place where this or that catastrophe occurs becomes a terrible and inseparable witness thereof; and the absence of silent characters of this sort would make the greatest scenes of history incomplete in the drama."

Though it would be ridiculous to pretend that Victor Hugo had the aesthetics of modern stage decoration in mind when he dashed off this foreword to "Cromwell," the fact remains that, without meaning to, he did stumble upon two observations which, since the advent of the so-called New Movement, have been taken more or less for granted by both audiences and designers. Night after night we sit before productions in which—in Hugo's words—the settings of our scenic artists, who are worthy of the name, contribute vitally to the pleasures of the evening by functioning not only as "inseparable witnesses" of the action but as "silent characters" in the drama that is being acted.

These visualizations of the playwright's world speak as eloquently to the eyes of their beholders as does the dramatist for whom they speak to the ears of those who listen to his words. In terms of line and color, but above all else in terms of the selection which betrays the talents of their creators, they give form and substance to what is at once significant and atmospheric, individual and emphatic in the little realm which, for a few brief hours, the playwright has staked off as his own and to which we, as members of the audience, are anxious to surrender as the most willing of willing subjects.

What we are apt to forget in a theatre that has so high a standard of visual competence as our own, is that this very competence was once a new idea which was worth fighting for and that the frequent lack of inspiration in our stage settings of to-day is due not to the designers who have fashioned them, but to the dictaphonic playwrights and the unimaginative theatre-goers who refuse to grant these scenic artists opportunities which are worthy of their best talents.

When the so-called New Movement first touched these shores, our stages

37

were set by hacks who devoted their lives to painting wings and backdrops in perspective, and to turning out interiors and exteriors which were so devoid of dramatic sense and sympathy that to understand their worthlessness, those of us who have been reared in a different tradition are nowadays compelled to consult the back files of such a vanished periodical as "The Theatre." Then, and only then, can those of us whose sole knowledge of the older settings is derived from their survival on the stages of small town stock companies or in the cheaper vaudeville houses, claim to have any comprehension of what scenery in this country was like before it took advantage of the vivid palettes of the distinguished Russian artists who at the turn of the century were treating their backdrops like glorified canvases, and of the selective and revolutionary theories of such all-important men as Craig and Appia.

When the New Movement first reached this country it was really new. It came as a challenge, was hot with protest, and possessed that magical contagion which invites alignments. It found the theatre divided against itself, with the younger men eager to respond to its new doctrines, and the older ones looking upon them with the distrust with which age and caution are always ready to welcome innovation. To them they seemed unnecessary, slightly ridiculous and somewhat seditious, in as much as they stressed the importance of such upstart crows as the director, and, even more especially, the designer.

There can be no denying that on several occasions our newly recruited designers did allow their sense of self-importance to go to their heads. As they experimented with color and with Cubism, with Impressionism and Expressionism, with stylized settings and with Constructivism, they undoubtedly did declare their occasional scene-maker's holidays at the expense of the plays which they were setting and the actors with whom they were working. But their rebellious attitude was on the whole as healthy as it was natural, and hastened, as nothing else could, the changes in production standards which these scenic artists were determined to effect.

The first days of excitement over such designs as Joseph Urban's backings for "The Love of Three Kings," or Mr. Jones's "The Man Who Married A Dumb Wife," or Mr. Simonson's "Maître Patelin" have long since passed. So, too, have those post-war years of breathless expectancy in the theatre when Mr. Jones won admiration for his beautiful settings for "The Jest," "Richard III," and "Hamlet"; when Mr. Geddes, who dreamed the magnificent dream his "Dante Project" represents, was experimenting with sculptural stages, and Mr.

Simonson was helping to add lustre to the beginnings of the Theatre Guild by his backgrounds for "The Faithful," "Liliom" and "Back to Methuselah."

To the ranks of the designers already mentioned, and to such of their contemporaries as Aline Bernstein, Livingston Platt, Raymond Sovey, Cleon Throckmorton and Woodman Thompson, has come a second generation of scenic artists, headed by Jo Mielziner and Donald Oenslager, to whom a third generation is even now about to be added, with Albert Johnston as its already established leader. The New Movement is, in other words, old and the points for which it battled are now as dead as only victorious causes in art can be. But because of these men and women, and the high gifts they have brought the theatre, our contemporary stage is a far more stimulating and satisfying place than it would ever have been if they had not believed in themselves as artists, and if as artists they had not succeeded in having their say behind the footlights.

Where they were once unruly and the theatre they served was vibrantly experimental, they have fitted into the working needs of a theatre which is more conforming and which, for the present, seems to be animated by a credo that is no more exciting than the hope for success which the good production of a good play almost invariably wins. They are the willing and devoted servants of the plays they are called in to design. The blame is not theirs but the playwrights for whom they work, if they are forced so frequently to squander their talents on shabby kitchens and middle class interiors, or to function as second-rate interior decorators.

The best of them—as Mr. Jones has shown in "The Green Bay Tree," and Mr. Geddes in "The Patriot," and Mr. Simonson in "The Apple Cart," and Mr. Mielziner in "The Barretts of Wimpole Street," and Mr. Oenslager in "Forsaking All Others"—have managed to add silent characters to the *dramatis personae* and inseparable witnesses to the action even when they have had to bridle their imaginations to the factual demands of playwrights. Oddly enough, and in spite of all rumors to the contrary, the best plays of the last fifteen or twenty years are vitally connected with the work of the best designers.

But being artists, these men and women are entitled to their dreams. To find a release in a theatre of their own imagining, they have been compelled to escape into a world where they could design unhampered by the limitations of literal scripts, cautious managers, and unimaginative playgoers. Their dreams have taken the form of projects such as these newly fashioned ones which are included in this exhibition.

39

Dreams they *may* be, but they spring from discontent, an inner compulsion to state an ideal, and a capacity for living beyond the present. As projects they are hopes unrealized. But their chances of ever reaching realization depend first of all upon their having been hopes. By being stated on paper, they gain a special significance because they envisage the theatre of the present as some of its ablest servitors see it in their minds' eyes. They may for that very reason point to its future. As Mr. Shaw said when he concluded his introduction to the Shaw-Terry Letters, "Let those who may complain that it was all on paper remember that only on paper has humanity yet achieved glory, beauty, truth, knowledge, virtue, and abiding love."

CATALOG

INDEX OF ARTISTS WITH CATALOG NUMBERS

THEATRE ART OF THE RENAISSANCE AND BAROQUE

The designers are arranged chronologically. *An asterisk indicates that the item is illustrated by a plate bearing the same number.

SIXTEENTH CENTURY

SERLIO, Sebastiano (1473–1554)   ITALIAN
  Born in Bologna, active there and in Venice; called to France by Francis I to work at his court; died at Fontainebleau.

  1 *DE ARCHITECTURA LIBRI QUIN-QUE*, Venice, 1569
        Lent by Mrs. Edith Isaacs, New York
  1A—Same work, English edition, 1611
      Lent by R. Hall, Tonbridge Wells, England
  2 Setting for a comedy: after an engraving in Serlio's *DE ARCHITECTURA;* model by Mrs. Lee Simonson
        Lent by the Dartmouth College Theatre Museum, Hanover, New Hampshire

PRIMATICCIO, Francesco (1504–1570)
                                    ITALIAN
  Born in Bologna, active in Mantua; called to France by Francis I and worked there until his death.
  Eight costume drawings:
  3 —Pageant costume
  4 —Pageant costume
  5 —Allegorical personage for court pageant
  6 —Fame, allegorical personage for court pageant
  7 —Roman Knight
  8 —Warrior
  *9 —Hermes and a Mourning Woman (Eurydice?)

*10 —Knight of the Swan
        Lent by the National Museum, Stockholm

BUONTALENTI, Bernardo (1536–1608)
                                    ITALIAN
  Born in Florence, active principally there, as well as in Pisa and Siena. His ingenious use of fireworks won for him the nick-name "Bernardo delle Girandole."

  SIX INTERLUDES, Florence, 1589:

  11 —The Music of the Spheres (engraved by Agostino Carracci)
  12 —Contest between the Fairies and the Muses (engraved by Epifanio d'Alfano)
  13 —Combat between Apollo and the Serpent Python (engraved by Agostino Carracci)
  14 —Appearance of Demons of Heaven and Hell (engraved by Epifanio d'Alfano)
  15 —Arion the Cither Player (engraved by Epifanio d'Alfano)
  16 —The Dance is a Gift of the Gods (engraved by Epifanio d'Alfano)
        Lent by the National Museum, Stockholm

RICCIUS SENENSIS   ITALIAN

*17 *ORTENSIO;* engraving, by Hieronymus Bols, of setting, Siena, 1589
        Lent by the National Museum, Stockholm

SEVENTEENTH CENTURY

JONES, Inigo (1573–1652)   ENGLISH
  Born in London, studied in Italy; worked at the court theatre in Denmark; architect and theatrical designer under James I and Charles I of England; appointed surveyor-general of public buildings in 1615. See section *The Masque Designs of Inigo Jones*, p. 22.

18 MASQUE OF BLACKNESSE (?), Ben Jonson; possibly a drawing for setting of first scene, "consisting of small woods and here and there a void place filled with huntings." *The Masque of Blacknesse* was presented on January 7, 1605. Chatsworth, No. 400: Border and Scene with a Stag Hunt

*19 THE MASQUE OF QUEENS, Ben Jonson; drawing for setting, Scene II; presented, February 2, 1609. Chatsworth, No. 17

OBERON, THE FAERY PRINCE, Ben Jonson; a masque for Prince Henry, presented, January 1, 1611: two drawings for settings:

*20 —Scene I, "Nothing perceiv'd but a darke Rocke with trees beyond it; and all wildness that could be presented. Till above the Horizon, the Moon began to shew, and rising, a Satyre was seen (by her light) to put forth head and call." Chatsworth, No. 40

*21 —Alternate drawing for Scene I; Chatsworth, No. 44

22 BRITTANIA TRIUMPHANS, Sir William Davenant; drawing for setting, Scene II: A Horrid Hell; presented, January 7, 1638. Chatsworth No. 260

*23 LUMINALIA or FESTIVAL OF LIGHT, Sir William Davenant (?); drawing for setting, Scene I: Night; presented, February 6, 1638. Chatsworth, No. 308

Nos. 18 to 23 lent by the Duke of Devonshire, Chatsworth

SABBATTINI, Nicola   ITALIAN

23A PRACTICA DI FABRICAR SCENE (*Technique of Making Theatre Settings*), 1637

Lent by J. Kyrle Fletcher, Ltd., Newport, England

VIGARANI, Carlo   ITALIAN

24 Drawing for setting of an opera, Paris, ca. 1660

Lent by the National Museum, Stockholm

24A Drawing of the proscenium of the "Salle des Machines," Tuileries, Paris, ca. 1670

Lent by the Tessin Collection, Drottningholm

*25-26 ATIS, Lully; two drawings for settings, Paris, 1675

26-27 THESEUS, Lully; two drawings for settings, Paris, 1675

28 ALCESTIS, Lully; drawing for setting, Paris, 1675

29 Drawing for setting of an opera, Paris, ca. 1675

Nos. 25–29 lent by the National Museum, Stockholm

VIGARANI (School)

30 Drawing of setting, Colonnade with Statues, Paris, late XVIIth century

Lent by the National Museum, Stockholm

ITALIAN SCHOOL (Anonymous)

31 Four drawings, designs for side scenes

32 Four drawings, designs for side wings

33 Drawing, design for stage equipment with backdrop on rollers

Lent by the National Museum, Stockholm

BÉRAIN, JEAN   FRENCH

Born in St. Mihiel, Lorraine; in 1674 received royal appointment and was commissioned by King Louis XIV to design decorations and costumes for court festivals and ceremonies.

34 ARMIDA, Lully; drawing for setting, Paris, ca. 1680

35 HESIONE; drawing for setting, Paris, ca. 1701

Nos. 34–35 lent by the National Museum, Stockholm

BÉRAIN, Jean and DOLIVET   FRENCH

Three drawings for settings, created in Paris in 1699 and sent to Stockholm for the theatre of Charles XII:

36 —Setting for comedies: village

37 —Setting for comedies: village
38 —Setting for serious pastorals
Lent by the National Museum, Stockholm

BÉRAIN (School)

Two costume drawings, ca 1690:
39 —Shepherdess
40 —Shepherd or Gardener
Lent by the National Museum, Stockholm

FRENCH SCHOOL (Anonymous)

41 Drawing for setting, late XVIIth century
42 Drawing for setting, ca. 1700
Lent by the National Museum, Stockholm

IUVARA, Filippo (1676?–1736)   ITALIAN

Born in Messina, studied in Rome under Carlo Fontana; became architect for King of Sicily. Active in Turin, Mantua, Milan, Rome and Portugal. Called to Madrid by Philip V in 1735 and died there the following year.

Two drawings for settings, Rome, 1706:
*43 —Open Heavens with Phoebus on High
44 —Piazza Prepared for Nocturnal Illumination with Triumphal Arch and Chariot
Lent by the National Museum, Stockholm

BIBIENA FAMILY (Galli da Bibiena)

A family which for over a hundred years was pre-eminent in designing for the theatre. They were employed at most of the principal courts in the late XVIIth and XVIIIth centuries and were instrumental in spreading the Italian Late Baroque style throughout Europe.
45 Drawing for setting, unidentified play
Lent by Mrs. Edith Isaacs, New York
46 Drawing for setting, unidentified play
Lent by the Duke of Devonshire, Chatsworth

BIBIENA, Giuseppe Galli (1696–1756)

Studied with his father, Ferdinando, and succeeded him in the service of the Archduke of Vienna. Active principally in Aus-

tria and Germany, died in Berlin while working for Frederick II.
Two drawings for settings:
47 —Interior
*48 —Ancient City
Lent by the National Museum, Stockholm

WACHSMUTH and others   GERMAN(?)
49 Child's Theatre, about 1730–1740: five colored engravings on cardboard, comprising four miniature wings and borders with actors, and one backdrop, set in a grooved wooden stage; engraved by Martin Engelbrecht after designs by Wachsmuth and others. The original series consisted of 189 pieces in 31 sets, together with a proscenium.
Lent by Lee Simonson, New York

MONTENARI, Giovanni   ITALIAN
49A DEL TEATRO OLIMPICO DE ANDREA PALLADIO IN VINCENZA; second edition, Padua, 1749
Lent by J. Kyr.'e Fletcher, Ltd., Newport, England

DE LA JOUE, Jacques (1687–1761)   FRENCH
Active in Paris as painter and designer under the patronage of Mme. de Pompadour and Louis XV.

50 Theatrical composition, ca. 1740
Lent by the Tessin Collection, Drottningholm
51 Another version of the same composition
Lent by the National Museum, Stockholm

RÈ, Vincenzo   ITALIAN
52 Drawing for a setting, Prison, ca. 1750
Lent by the National Museum, Stockholm

? GALLIARI, Fabrizio (1709–1790)   ITALIAN
Collaborated with his brother Bernardino at Turin; later worked at the Court Theatre, Vienna. Returned to Italy and was active in Bergamo, Turin and Treviglio.
*53 Drawing for setting, A Cortile, ca. 1775
Lent by the National Museum, Stockholm

CHALLE, Michelange Charles (1718–1778)
FRENCH

Architect and mathematician, active in Paris in the XVIIIth century.

54 Design for setting, Paris, ca. 1770
Lent by the Theatre Museum, Drottningholm

55 *ARMIDA* (?), Glück; design for setting, last act, Paris, ca. 1775
Lent by the Theatre Museum, Drottningholm

THE FAMILY BOQUET, French, late 18th century

56–63 Eight costume drawings for the Royal Opera, Stockholm, ca. 1775: Shepherd, Muse, Venus, Princess, Adonis, Cleopatra, Queen of Egypt, Asmenias, Priest sent by the Gods, Apollo
Lent by the Royal Opera, Stockholm

XAVERY, C. J.   DUTCH

63A *HET ITALIAANSCH TOONEEL (The Italian Stage);* ca. 1770
Lent by J. Kyrle Fletcher, Ltd., Newport, England

DESPRÉZ, Louis Jean (1743–1804)   FRENCH
Born in Auxerre, worked as painter and architect in Paris and Lyon. While travelling in Italy he met King Gustavus III and returned with him to Stockholm where he was employed until his death as architect, sculptor, painter and designer for plays and festivals.

*64 *QUEEN CHRISTINE;* drawing for setting, Act I, Gripsholm, 1784

65–71 Seven sketches for settings and properties, ca. 1785

72 *GUSTAF WASA,* Naumann; drawing for setting, Stockholm, 1786

73–75 *GUSTAF WASA,* Naumann; three costume drawings, Stockholm, 1786

76–77 *GUSTAF ADOLF AND EBBA BRAHE,* Gustavus III and Kellgren; two drawings for settings, Stockholm, 1788

78 *GUSTAF ADOLF AND EBBA BRAHE,* Gustavus III and Kellgren; costume drawing, Stockholm, 1788
Nos. 64–78 lent by the National Museum, Stockholm

AENEAS IN CARTHAGE, Gustavus III and Kellgren; six drawings for settings, Stockholm, 1799:

79 —Prologue, Rock of Aeolus
80 —Prologue, The Fleet of the Trojans
81 —Scenes
82 —Scene
83 —Scene
84 —Scene

85 Drawing for setting, unidentified
Nos. 79 to 85 lent by the National Museum, Stockholm

LAMBERTI, Vincenzo   ITALIAN
85A *LA REGOLATA CONSTRUZION DE' TEATRI (Rules for the Construction of Theatres);* first edition, Naples, 1787
Lent by J. Kyrle Fletcher, Ltd., Newport, England

PIONEERS OF MODERN THEATRE ART
SAXE-MEININGEN, APPIA, AND CRAIG

DUKE GEORGE II OF SAXE-MEININGEN
Duke George II, 1826–1914, made Meiningen the center of progress in the theatre arts during the period 1870–90; see page 17.

86 *DON GIOVANNI,* Mozart; costume drawing for Masetto and Leporello
THE MAID OF ORLEANS, Schiller; two costume drawings:
87 —Lionel

88 —An Archer
Nos. 86 to 88 lent by the Cologne Theatre Museum

THE MAID OF ORLEANS, Schiller, four drawings for settings:
89A —Before Reims, without actors
89B —Before Reims, with actors
90A —Skirmish in woods
90B —Joan captured
Lent by the Civic Museum, Meiningen

91 THE PRETENDERS, Björnson; drawing for costumes of Norwegian Peasants
Lent by the Cologne Theatre Museum

*92 THE PRETENDERS, Björnson; drawing for setting
Lent by the Civic Museum, Meiningen
93 Costume drawing, male character, unidentified play
Lent by the Cologne Theatre Museum

HERMANNSCHLACHT; two drawings for settings:
94 —Without actors
*95 —With actors
Lent by the Civic Museum, Meiningen

APPIA, Adolphe   SWISS
Born in Geneva 1862; died in Zurich 1928. Worked chiefly in Switzerland, Germany and France; for many years associated with Jacques Dalcroze at Hellerau. See page 18.

THE VALKYRIE, Wagner; two drawings for settings, 1892:
96 —Act III, finale
97 —The Sleep of Brunhilde
Lent by the Estate of Adolphe Appia through the courtesy of the Museum of Art and History, Geneva

THE VALKYRIE, Wagner, three models for settings.
98 —Act I, scene 1
99 —Act II, scene 1
100 —Act III, scene 1
Lent by the Cologne Theatre Museum

THE RHEINGOLD, Wagner; drawing for setting, 1892:
101 —Valhalla
Lent by the Estate of Adolphe Appia through the courtesy of the Museum of Art and History, Geneva

THE RHEINGOLD, Wagner, three models for settings:
102 —Act I, scene 1
103 —Acts II and IV
104 —Act III, scene 1
Lent by the Cologne Theatre Museum

PARSIFAL, Wagner; three drawings for settings, 1896:
*105 —Act I: The Sacred Forest
*106 —Act II: Klingsor's Dungeon
107 —Act III: The Flowering Meadow
Lent by the Estate of Adolphe Appia through the courtesy of the Museum of Art and History, Geneva

Three rhythmic designs, 1909(?), for the Dalcroze Theatre, Hellerau
*108 —The Cataracts of the Dawn
109 —The Forest
*110 —Rhythmic Composition
Lent by M. Jacques Dalcroze, Geneva

TRISTAN AND ISOLDE, Wagner; four drawings for settings, 1923:
111 —Act II, Opening Scene
112 —Act II, Isolde Extinguishes the Torch
113 —Act II, The Arrival of King Mark
114 —Act II, Finale

LITTLE EYOLF, Ibsen; drawing for setting, 1924:
115 —Act II

IPHIGENIA IN AULIS, Glück; four drawings for settings, 1926:
116 —Act I, Scene 1
117 —Act I, Scene 2
118 —Act II
119 —Act III

KING LEAR, Shakespeare; two drawings for settings, 1926:

120 —Acts I and II
121 —Act III

ORPHEUS, Glück; drawing for setting, 1926:

122 —Descent to Hades

Nos. 111 to 122 lent by the Estate of Adolphe Appia through the courtesy of the Museum of Art and History, Geneva

CRAIG, Edward Gordon   Eɴɢʟɪsʜ

Born near London, 1872; has worked chiefly in London and Florence.

*123–*134 Settings for an Ideal Theatre, twelve etchings, 1907

"These etchings were made by the artist in the Spring of 1907 at Florence and represent his most serious work. Connected as they are with his dream of an Ideal Theatre, they in no way have anything in common with the modern stage." (From the foreword to the portfolio in which these etchings were issued)

Lent by Alfred Stieglitz, New York

AUSTRIA

BAHNER, Willi   Vɪᴇɴɴᴀ

TWELFTH NIGHT, Shakespeare; five drawings for settings, Civic Theatre, Vienna, 1929:

135 —Hall of the Duke
136 —Street Scene
137 —The Harbor
138 —Olivia's Garden
139 —Room in Olivia's House

140 CENODOXUS, DOCTOR OF PARIS, drawing for setting of Finale, Civic Theatre, Vienna, 1933

Nos. 135–140 lent by the Artist

BESCHORNER, Irmgard Dʀᴇsᴅᴇɴ, Vɪᴇɴɴᴀ

141 MEASURE FOR MEASURE, Shakespeare; drawing for setting of Act V

142–144 ——————, O'Neill (?); three drawings for settings

Nos. 141–144 lent by the Artist

STRNAD, Oscar   Vɪᴇɴɴᴀ

KING LEAR, Shakespeare; two drawings for settings, Josefstadter Theatre, 1920–1927, director Reinhardt:

*145 —Gloucester's Castle
145A—Lear before the House of Goneril

146–149 HAMLET, Shakespeare; four drawings for settings, People's Theatre, Vienna, 1922

*150–155 DANTON'S DEATH, Georg Büchner; six drawings for settings, People's Theatre, Amsterdam, 1922

156–167 JULIUS CAESAR, Shakespeare; twelve projects for settings, 1922

168 MIDSUMMER NIGHT'S DREAM, Shakespeare; drawing for setting, 1927, director Reinhardt

Nos. 145–168 lent by the Artist

CZECHOSLOVAKIA

HEYTHUM, A.   Pʀᴀɢᴜᴇ

*169 DESIRE UNDER THE ELMS, O'Neill; drawing for setting, constructed in stepped stages of which only the part where action occurs is lighted, State National Theatre, Prague, 1925, director K. Dostal

THE GREAT GOD BROWN, O'Neill; two drawings for settings, State National Theatre, Prague, 1928, director K. Dostal:

*170 —Brown's Office
*171 —Scene by the Sea

MERCHANT OF VENICE Shakespeare; four drawings for settings, State National Theatre, Prague, 1930, director K. Dostal:

*172 —Street in Venice
173 —Ghetto
174 —Shylock's House
175 —Belmont

176 THE FATAL PLAY OF LOVE, Capek; drawing for setting, State National Theatre, Prague, 1930, director J. Frejka

ALADDIN, Klococ; three drawings for settings, State National Theatre, Prague, 1933, director K. Dostal:

177 —Scene in a Bank
178 —Scene in a Casino
179 —Attic-room in a Slum
Nos. 169–179 lent by the Artist

HOFMAN, Vlastislav   PRAGUE
180 THE MAN WHO WAS THURSDAY, Chesterton; drawing for setting, State National Theatre, Prague, 1922, director K. Dostal

181 CHRISTINA, Strindberg; drawing for setting, State National Theatre, Prague, 1922, director Hilar

182 THE GAME OF LOVE AND DEATH, Rolland; drawing for setting, State National Theatre, Prague, 1925, director Hilar

183 ANTIGONE, Sophocles; drawing for setting, State National Theatre, Prague, 1925, director K. Dostal

*184–*185 HAMLET, Shakespeare; four draw-
*186   ings for settings, State National Thea-
*187   tre, Prague, 1926, director Hilar

*188 THE DICTATOR, Romains; drawing for setting, State National Theatre, Prague, 1927, director Hilar

189–191 THE DEMON, Dostoievski; three drawings for settings, State National Theatre, Prague, 1929, director K. Dostal

192 ELIZABETH OF ENGLAND, Bruckner; drawing for setting, State National Theatre, Prague, 1929, director Hilar

*193–194 R. U. R., Capek; two drawings for settings, State National Theatre, Prague, 1929, director Kodicak

195–196 MARCO MILLIONS, O'Neill; two drawings for settings, Municipal Theatre, Prague, 1930, director J. Bor

197 AMPHITRYON, Giraudoux; drawing for setting, State National Theatre, Prague, 1931, director Hilar

198A–198B OEDIPUS, Sophocles; two drawings for settings, State National Theatre, Prague, 1931–1932, director Hilar

199A–199B EMPEROR JONES, O'Neill; two drawings for settings, Municipal Theatre, Prague, director Bor
Nos. 180 to 199 lent by the Artist

200 CRIME AND PUNISHMENT, Dostoievski; drawing for setting, Municipal Theatre, Prague, director Bor
Lent by the Municipal Theatre, Prague

DENMARK

NIELSEN, Kay   COPENHAGEN
201 ALLADIN, drawing for setting, 1917: Proscenium

ALLADIN, two drawings for costumes, 1917:

202A —Hindu Dancer

202B —Chinese Fiddler with Drum
Nos. 201 to 202B lent by Leicester Square Galleries, London

ENGLAND

BLANCH, Mrs. Lesley   LONDON

203 *AMPHITRYON*, Molière; drawing for setting

AMPHITRYON, Molière; four drawings for costumes:
204 —Theban Captain
205 —Sosia
206 —Jupiter
207 —Alcmena

*208 *THE MERCHANT OF VENICE*, Shakespeare; Shakespeare Memorial Theatre, Stratford, 1932; Komisarzhevsky director; drawing for permanent setting

*209 *THE MERCHANT OF VENICE*, Shakespeare; drawing for costume, 1932: Shylock

210 *ROUGE ET NOIR;* drawing for costume: The King
Nos. 203 to 210 lent by the Artist

CRAIG, Edward Gordon: See *Pioneers of Modern Theatre Art*, page 46

DEXEL, Walter   LONDON
MANN IST MANN, Bert Brecht, produced in Germany; two drawings for settings
211 —Act II, Pagoda
212 —Act V
Lent by Dr. Adolf Behne, Berlin
Courtesy the Artist

FRASER, C. Lovat   LONDON
213 Drawing for a permanent setting for Eighteenth Century comedy

214 *MUCH ADO ABOUT NOTHING*, Shakespeare; drawing for costume: Court Lady

215 *AS YOU LIKE IT*, Shakespeare; drawing for setting: Forest of Arden

216 *THE BEGGARS' OPERA*, John Gay; drawing for costume, 1920: Lady of the Town

217 *PILGRIM'S PROGRESS;* drawing for costume, 1920: Devil

218 *THE TEMPEST*, Shakespeare; drawing for setting, 1921: Act II, Scene 1, Another Part of the Island

219 *THE TEMPEST*, Shakespeare; drawing for costume, 1921: A Strange Shape

220 *MACBETH*, Shakespeare; drawing for costume, 1921: Witch

221 *THE DEVIL IS AN ASS*, Ben Jonson; drawing for costume, 1921: Pug, the Lesser Devil

222 *CROSSINGS*, Walter de la Mare; drawing for costume, 1921: An African Fairy
Nos. 213 to 222 lent by Mrs. Lovat Fraser

JONES, Inigo: See section *Theatre Art of the Renaissance and Baroque Periods*, page 43

MESSEL, Oliver   LONDON
223 *THE MIRACLE*, director, Reinhardt; drawing for setting, 1932: A Tree

THE MIRACLE; three drawings for costumes, 1932:
224 —Hungarian Dancer
225 —Huntsman
226 —Companion of Robber Count

227 *LA BELLE HÉLÈNE*, Offenbach, director, Reinhardt; drawing for drop-scene, 1932: Gods and Goddesses

LA BELLE HÉLÈNE, Offenbach; six drawings for costumes, 1932:
228 —Grecian Athlete
229 —Grecian Maiden
230 —Juno

231 —Bachis, Maid to Hélène
232 —Achilles
233 —Masked Chorus
　　　Nos. 223 to 233 lent by the Artist

RICKETTS, Charles　　　LONDON
233A-B *MACBETH*, Shakespeare; two draw-
　　ings for settings
　　　Lent by Martin Birnbaum, New York

RUTHERSTON, Albert　　　OXFORD
　　THE WINTER'S TALE, Shakespeare;
　　four drawings for costumes, 1912:
234 —Courtier
235 —Country Girl
236 —Morris Dancers, man and woman
　　　Lent by Lillah McCarthy, O.B.E.
　　　　(Lady Keeble), London

237 *THE WINTER'S TALE*, Shakespeare;
　　two drawings for costumes, 1912:
　　Clown and Country Girl
　　　Lent by Kenneth Clark, Oxford

238 *THE DOCTOR'S DILEMNA*, Shaw;
　　drawing for costume, 1913: Jennifer
　　　Lent by the Artist

　　LE REVEIL DE FLORE, Pavlova ballet;
　　two drawings for costumes, 1914:
239 —Costume for Pavlova
　　　Lent by the Ashmolean Museum, Oxford

240 —Dancer
　　　Lent by the Artist

241 *ANDROCLES AND THE LION*, Shaw;
　　drawing for costume: Masked Slave
　　　Lent by Lillah McCarthy, O.B.E.,
　　　　(Lady Keeble), London

SHERINGHAM, George　　　LONDON
242 *THE TEMPEST*, Shakespeare; drawing
　　for backdrop

243 *TWELFTH NIGHT*, Shakespeare; draw-
　　ing for curtain, 1932: Street Scene
　　　Nos. 242, 243 lent by the Artist

WILKINSON, Norman　　　LONDON
　　A MIDSUMMER NIGHT'S DREAM,
　　Shakespeare; four drawings for cos-
　　tumes, 1913:
244 —Puck
245 —Flute as Thisbe
246 —Moonshine
247 —Attendant
　　　Lent by the Artist

　　LOVE'S LABOUR'S LOST, Shakespeare;
　　two drawings for costumes:
248 —Scene of Taking the Oath
249 —Braggart and Page
　　　Lent by Mrs. Arthur Heaton, Birming-
　　　　ham, England

250 *THE TROJAN WOMEN*, Euripides;
　　drawing for costume, 1915: Chorus
251 *IPHIGENIA IN TAURIS*, Euripides;
　　drawing for costume, 1915: Men Tem-
　　ple Attendants
　　　Nos. 250 to 251 lent by the Artist

ZINKEISEN, Doris　　　LONDON
　　C. B. Cochran revue, 1929; three drawings
　　for costumes of the period of 1900:
252 —Shiela Wilson
*253 —Jane Welsh
254 —Iris Brown
　　　Lent by the Artist

　　NYMPH ERRANT, James Laver; four
　　drawings for costumes of the period of
　　1830:
255 —Mrs. Jones
256 —Mrs. Huntington
257 —La Marchesa Bantalina
258 —Miss Corneille Marcon
　　　Lent by C. B. Cochran, London

FINLAND

WARÉN, Matti　　　HELSINGFORS
259-260 *I AM GUILTY: A DRAMA OF
SAUL AND DAVID*, Maria Jothini;
two drawings for settings, Finnish National Theatre, Helsingfors, 1929
　　　Lent by the Artist

FRANCE

AND THE SCHOOL OF PARIS

In this section is included the work of many non-French designers who live in Paris. Other French designers are included in the section: Theatre Art of the Renaissance and Baroque Periods

BAKST, Léon
> Born in Russia, 1868; died in Paris, 1924.

261 *SADKO*, Rimsky-Korsakoff, 1911; drawing for costume: Boyar
> *Lent by Mrs. E. C. MacVeagh, New York*

262 *GOOD-HUMORED LADIES*, D. Scarlatti, Russian Ballet, Rome, 1917; drawing for costume: Constanza
> *Lent by M. Knoedler and Company, New York*

GOOD-HUMORED LADIES, D. Scarlatti, Russian Ballet; three drawings for costumes:

263 —Battista
264 —Mariuccia
265 —Mendiant

266 *THE SLEEPING PRINCESS*, Tchaikowsky, Russian Ballet, London, 1922; drawing for setting: The Baptism Scene
Nos. 263 to 266 lent by Mrs. John W. Garrett, Baltimore, Maryland

LE MARTYRE DE SAINT-SÉBASTIEN, Paris, 1922; two drawings for costumes:
*267 —(?) Prince with Negro Page
268 —Mesopotamian Dignitary
> *Lent by Mrs. E. C. MacVeagh, New York*

269 *SCHÉHÉRAZADE*, Rimsky-Korsakoff, Russian Ballet, Paris, 1910; drawing for setting
> *Lent by George Blumenthal, New York*

BARSACQ, André   PARIS
*270-272 *VOLPONE*, Ben Jonson; three drawings for settings, 1928; Théâtre de l'Atelier, Paris

VOLPONE, Ben Jonson; four drawings for costumes, 1928:

273 —Leone, Captain of the Fleet
*274 —Magistrate
275 —Soldier
276 —Valet

277 *THE BEAUX' STRATEGEM*, George Farquhar; drawing for setting, 1930: Act II, Balcony of the House

THE BEAUX' STRATEGEM, George Farquhar; three drawings for costumes, 1930:

278 —Count
279 —Lady
280 —Innkeeper

281 *THE SON OF DON JUAN* (?), José Echegaray; three drawings for settings

THE RAPE OF LUCRECE, André Obey; three drawings for costumes, 1931:

282 —Collatine
283 —Tarquin
284 —The Narrator
> *Nos. 270 to 284, lent by the Artist*

BRAQUE, Georges   PARIS
285 *LES FACHEUX*, Auric, Swedish Ballet, Paris, 1924; model for setting
> *Lent by Paul Rosenberg, Paris*

de CHIRICO, Giorgio: see Italian section

DERAIN, André   PARIS
286 *LA BOUTIQUE FANTASQUE*; Rossini-Respighi, Russian Ballet, London, 1919; drawing for curtain
> *Lent by Paul Rosenberg, Paris*

DOBUZHINSKY, Mstislav: see U. S. S. R. section

FUERST, Walter René   PARIS

THE EMPEROR JONES, Eugene
O'Neill; three drawings for settings,
1923:

287 —Forest
288 —At the Foot of a Great Tree
289 —Throne Room
290-291 THE ORESTEIA, Aeschylus; two
drawings for settings

THE ORESTEIA, Aeschylus; three drawings for costumes:

292 —Clytemnestra
293 —Aegisthus
294 —Taltubios
Nos. 287 to 294 lent by the Artist

GOLOVINE, Alexander: see U.S.S.R. section

GONTCHAROVA, Nathalie   PARIS

Born in Russia 1881, has worked in Paris
since c. 1914.

LITURGY, Russian Ballet, Lausanne,
1915; three reproductions of drawings
for costumes:

295 —The Apostle Andrew
296 —The Apostle Matthew
*297 —Cherub
297A LITURGY, drawing for setting

ESPAGNE, Ravel, Russian Ballet, Rome,
1916; two drawings for costumes:

298 —Man
299 —Woman
*Nos. 295 to 299 lent by Mrs. S. Bashkiroff,
New York*

300 COQ D'OR, Rimsky-Korsakoff, Russian
Ballet, Paris, 1914; drawing
*Lent by the Bakrushin Theatre Museum,
Moscow*

LAGUT, Irène   PARIS

301 LES MARIÉS DE LA TOUR EIFFEL,
Swedish Ballet, Rolf de Maré, producer,
1921; drawing for setting
*Lent by Les Archives Internationales de la
Danse, Paris*

LARIONOFF, Michael   PARIS

Born in Russia; has worked in Paris since
c. 1914.

302 RENARD, Stravinski, Russian Ballet,
Paris, 1922; drawing for setting

RENARD, Stravinski, Russian Ballet;
three drawings for costumes:

303 —Pilgrim
304 —Nun
305 —Peasant
Nos. 302 to 305 lent by the Artist

LÉGER, Fernand   PARIS

306-307 LA CRÉATION DU MONDE,
Swedish Ballet, Rolf de Maré, producer,
1923; two drawings for curtains
*Lent by Les Archives Internationales de la
Danse, Paris*

MEDGYES, Ladislas: see Hungarian section

PERDRIAT, Hélène   PARIS

308 LE MARCHAND D'OISEAUX, Swedish Ballet, Rolf de Maré, producer,
1923; drawing for setting
*Lent by Les Archives Internationales de la
Danse, Paris*

PICASSO, Pablo   PARIS

Born in Spain; has worked in Paris since
1899.

*309 PARADE, Russian Ballet, Paris, 1917;
drawing for a Chinese costume
Lent by Les Fils de Léon Helft, Paris

310 LE TRICORNE, Russian Ballet, London,
1920; drawing for curtain
Lent by Paul Rosenberg, Paris

CUADRO FLAMENCO, de Falla, Russian Ballet, Paris, 1921; two paintings,
originally parts of the curtain; painted
by Picasso himself:

*311 —Theatre Box, Lady and Gentleman, on
canvas, 76 x 57½ inches

312 —Theatre Box, Two Ladies, on canvas,
75¾ x 54 inches
Lent by Les Fils de Léon Helft, Paris

de SEGONZAC, André Dunoyer PARIS
LE MESSAGER, Henry Bernstein; three
drawings for settings:
313 —Act I, In Uganda
314 —Act II, Small Drawing-room in Paris
315 —Act III, A Smart Restaurant
Lent by the Artist

SOUDEIKINE, Sergei: see U. S. S. R. section

SURVAGE, Léopold PARIS
Born in Russia; has worked in Paris since
1908.

L'ÉCOLE DES FEMMES, Molière; four
drawings for settings, 1922:
316 —House of Agnès, with Plan of Setting

317 —House of Arnolphe, street side, House
of Arnolphe, garden side
Lent by the Artist

VAKALO, Georges PARIS
Born in Greece, works in Paris.
318 LIFE IS A DREAM, Calderón; drawing
for setting

LIFE IS A DREAM, Calderón; two
drawings for costumes:
319 —Rosaura
320 —Servant

THE PEACE, Aristophanes, Théâtre de
l'Atelier; six drawings for costumes:
321 —Tumult
322 —First Servant
323 —Coryphée
324 —Vase Merchant
325 —Vine-dresser
*326 —Le Bougier
Nos. 318 to 326 lent by the Artist

GERMANY

DANIEL, Heinz HAMBURG
*327 FAUST, Part I, Goethe; drawing for
setting, 1931
Lent by the Cologne Theatre Museum

PYGMALION, Shaw; drawing for setting, German State Theatre, Hamburg,
1932, director Günther Haenl:
328 —Setting for Acts III and V

329 COMEDY OF ERRORS, Shakespeare;
drawing for setting, German State Theatre, Hamburg, 1933

MACBETH, Verdi; drawing for setting,
State Opera, Hamburg, 1933, director
Fritz Oskar Schuh:
330 —Act II: A Hall
Nos. 328 to 330 lent by the Artist

GLIESE, Rochus ESSEN
DER BLAUE BOLL, Barlach; two drawings for settings, 1930:

331 —Scene 3
332 —Scene 7

THE PORTUGUESE BATTLE, Peuzoldt;
two drawings for settings, 1931:
333 —Penamakor
334 —The Widow's Residence

THE CROWD SEEKS, Neumeyer; two
drawings for settings, 1931:
335 —Setting for scenes 2, 3, 4, and 10
336 —Setting, Scene 7

337-339 THE CROWD SEEKS, Neumeyer;
three photographs of settings, 1931

KING CUCKOLD, Kaiser; two drawings
for settings, 1931:
340 —Setting for scenes 6, 7, 8, and 9
341 —Scene 11
Nos. 331 to 341 lent by the Artist

GRETE, Heinz NUREMBERG

342 EURYANTHE, Weber; drawing for setting

THE MEISTERSINGERS, Wagner; drawing for setting:

343 —Festival grounds

344 TANNHAÜSER, Wagner; drawing for setting

345 A MIDSUMMER NIGHT'S DREAM, Shakespeare; drawing for setting
Nos. 342–345 lent by the artist

GRÖNING, Karl

346 CARMEN, Bizet; drawing for setting, Act I, 1923

347 IPHIGENIA, Goethe; drawing for setting, Municipal Theatre, Altona, 1929

PYGMALION, Shaw; two drawings for settings, Municipal Theatre, Altona, 1930–1931:

348 —Setting for Act II
349 —Setting for Act III
Nos. 346 to 349 lent by the Cologne Theatre Museum

HECKROTH, Heinrich DÜSSELDORF

FAUST, Goethe; drawing for setting, 1931:

350 —A Gloomy Day, A Field

351 DAGMAR; drawing for setting, Act I, State Opera, Dresden, 1932

PEER GYNT, Ibsen; drawing for setting, Municipal Theatre, Essen:

352 —Scene: Lunatic Asylum

353 AIDA, Verdi; drawing for setting, Municipal Theatre, Essen

354 DER FREISCHÜTZ, Weber; drawing for setting, Municipal Theatre, Essen
Nos. 350–354 lent by the Cologne Theatre Museum

HELMDACH, Heinz MAGDEBURG

DER ROSENKAVALIER, Richard Strauss; drawing for setting, 1931:

355 —Room in the House of von Faninal

LOHENGRIN, Wagner; drawing for setting, 1932:

356 —Act II: Castle

357 KING FOR A DAY; drawing for setting, 1932

EGMONT, Goethe; drawing for setting, 1932:

358 —A Square in Brünel
Nos. 355–358 lent by the Artist

LOEFFLER, Edouard MANNHEIM

AIDA, Verdi; drawing for setting:

359 —Act III: The Banks of the Nile

*360 CARMEN, Bizet; drawing for setting

361 DON GIOVANNI, Mozart; drawing for setting

362 A MIDSUMMER NIGHT'S DREAM, Shakespeare; drawing for setting
Nos. 359 to 362 lent by the National Theatre, Mannheim

MAHNKE, Adolph DRESDEN

ELGA, Gerhart Hauptmann; drawing for setting, 1920:

363 —Scenes 1 and 6: Room in a Convent

364 GÖTZ VON BERLICHINGEN, Goethe; drawing for setting, State Theatre, Dresden, 1932, director Gielen

TROILUS AND CRESSIDA, Shakespeare; drawing for setting and photograph, State Theatre, Dresden:

365 —Act III, Scene 1: A Room in Priam's Palace

JULIUS CAESAR, Shakespeare; three drawings for settings with photographs, State Theatre, Dresden:

366 —Act I, Scenes 1 and 3; Act III, Scene 3: A Street in Rome

367 —Act II, Scene 1: Brutus' Orchard
368 —Act III, Scene 1: Before the Capitol
 *Nos. 363 to 368 lent by the Cologne
 Theatre Museum*

MEININGEN, Duke George II: see section
 Pioneers of Modern Theatre Art

MUELLER, Traugott BERLIN
 THE BRIDE OF MESSINA; two drawings for settings, Municipal Theatre,
 Berlin:
369 —Scene 1
370 —Scene 3

 THE NIBELUNGEN, Wagner; two drawings for settings:
371 —Act I, Scene 5
372 —Act I, Scene 6
 Nos. 369 to 372 lent by the Artist

PILARTZ, T. C. COLOGNE
373 *THE MAID OF ORLEANS*, Schiller;
 drawing for setting, Cologne Theatre,
 1932–1933, director Fritz Holl

 THE LUCK OF THE FILIBUSTERS;
 drawing for costumes, Cologne Theatre, 1932–1933:
374 —Three Pirates

 THE STREET WITHOUT AN END;
 drawing for setting, Cologne Theatre,
 1933:
375 —Act I
 *Nos. 373 to 375 lent by the Cologne
 Theatre Museum*

POELZIG, Hans BERLIN
376 *DON GIOVANNI*, Mozart; drawing for
 setting

377 *HAMLET*, Shakespeare; drawing for setting

 MUNKEN WENDT, Knut Hamsun; two
 drawings for settings:
378 —Act II
379 —Last Act
 Nos. 376 to 379 lent by the Artist

REIGBERT, Otto COLOGNE
 THE KING, Hanns Johst; drawing for
 four costumes, Kammerspiele, Munich,
 1919:
380 —Four costumes: Author; Plasterer; Two
 Builders

 FIESCO, Schiller; drawing for setting,
 Kammerspiele, Munich, 1920:
381 —Act I, Scene 5
382 *A MIDSUMMER NIGHT'S DREAM*,
 Shakespeare; drawing for setting, Kammerspiele, Munich, 1926
383 *THE DEATH OF DANTON*, Georg
 Büchner; drawing for setting, Kammerspiele, Munich, 1927
*384 *NACHFOLGE CHRISTI-SPIEL*, Max
 Mell, Kammerspiele, Munich; drawing
 for setting
385 *THRICE-DEAD PETER;* drawing for
 setting, Kammerspiele, Munich, 1927
 *Nos. 380 to 385 lent by the Cologne
 Theatre Museum*

SCHENK VON TRAPP, Lothar WIESBADEN
 THE FLYING DUTCHMAN, Wagner;
 three drawings for settings, with photographs of drawings and of completed
 settings:
386 —Act I: By the Sea
387 —Act II: Room in Daland's House
388 —Act III: Seashore near Daland's House

389–390 *ANGELINA*, Rossini; two drawings
 giving elevation and plan of setting, with
 photographs of completed setting
 Nos. 386 to 390 lent by the Artist

SAXE-MEININGEN, Duke George II: see section *Pioneers of Modern Theatre Art*

SCHROEDER, Johannes HAMBURG
 EMPEROR AND GALILEAN, Ibsen:
391 —Drawing for setting
392 —Photograph of setting
393–394 *EGMONT*, Goethe; two drawings
 for settings
 Nos. 391 to 394 lent by the Artist

56

SIEVERT, Ludwig   FRANKFORT

395 *JUDITH;* drawing for setting, Frankfort,
       1921, director Richard Weichert

*396 *THE BROAD HIGHWAY,* Strindberg;
       drawing for setting, Frankfort 1923,
       director Dr. Fritz Peter Buch

*397 *SALOME,* Richard Strauss; drawing for
       setting, 1925

398 *THE NIBELUNGEN,* Wagner; drawing
       for setting, Frankfort, 1925, director
       Dr. Lothar Wallerstein

399 *COSÍ FAN TUTTE,* Mozart; drawings
       for setting, Frankfort, Salzburg, State
       Opera, Vienna, director Dr. Lothar
       Wallerstein

400 *MACBETH,* Shakespeare; drawing for
       setting: Castle
                 Nos. 395 to 400 lent by the Artist

SOEHNLEIN, Kurt   HANOVER

401 *TURANDOT;* drawing for setting, 1929

402 *ORPHEUS,* Glück; drawing for setting,
       1930

*403 *MACBETH,* Shakespeare; drawing for
       setting, 1931
                 Nos. 401 to 403 lent by the Artist

SUHR, Edward   BERLIN

MISSISSIPPI, George Kaiser; drawing for
       setting, People's Theatre, Berlin, 1930:

404 —Scene I: Warehouse in New Orleans

OCTOBER EIGHTEENTH, Erich Walter
       Schäfer; drawing for setting, Schiller
       Theatre, Berlin, 1932:

405 —Battlefield near Leipzig, 1813

LA VALLIÈRE, Janos von Mory; draw-
       ing for setting, Schiller Theatre, Berlin,
       1933:

406 —Scene 5: Camp in Flanders, 1730

PRINCE FREDERICK OF HAMBURG,
       Heinrich von Kleist; drawing for setting,
       Hessian Regional Theatre, Darmstadt,
       1933:

407 —Courtyard of a Castle, Berlin
                 Nos. 404 to 407 lent by the Artist

TORSTEN, Axel
                           FRANKFORT AND KARLSRUHE

408 *BAYAZZO,* Leoncavallo; drawing for set-
       ting, State Theatre, Karlsruhe, 1929

THE FLYING DUTCHMAN, Wagner;
       drawing for setting, Suomalain Opera,
       Helsingfors:

409 —Act III: The Ghost Ship

409A *THE MARVELOUS MANDARIN,* R.
       Kreideweiss; drawing for setting, State
       Theatre, Karlsruhe, 1933

410 *THE MARVELOUS MANDARIN,* R.
       Kreideweiss; costume drawing, 1933

411 *THE GLASS PRINCESS;* costume draw-
       ing, 1933

412 *TEA COSY;* costume drawing, 1933

413 *THE CHEERFUL MYNHEER,* costume
       drawing, 1933
                 Nos. 408 to 413 lent by the Artist

WILDERMANN, Hans   BRESLAU

414 *DON JUAN AND FAUST,* Grabbe;
       drawing for setting, Municipal Thea-
       tre, Dortmund, 1919

415 *RIENZI,* Wagner; drawing for setting,
       Opera House, Hamburg, 1930

416 *GIANNI SCHICCHI,* Puccini; drawing
       for setting, Opera House, Breslau

417 *DER FREISCHÜTZ,* Weber; drawing
       for setting, Opera House, Breslau, 1932,
       director Dr. Hartmann

418 *BORIS GODUNOFF,* Moussorgsky; draw-
       ing for setting, Opera House, Breslau

419 *AMPHITRYON,* Heinrich von Kleist;
       drawing for setting, Municipal Thea-
       tre, Dortmund
                 *Nos. 414 to 419 lent by the
                 Cologne Theatre Museum*

HUNGARY

FÜLÖP, Zoltán   BUDAPEST

420 *IRJA HADNAGY*, drawing for setting, 1932; Studio Theatre, Budapest
  Lent by Charles Rosner, Budapest

MEDGYES, Ladislas PARIS AND BUDAPEST

421 *THE SEVEN SONGS*, Malipiero; model for setting; Théâtre des Mathurins, Paris, 1925

422 *CAESAR AND CLEOPATRA*, Shaw; three drawings for settings; Belvarosi Theatre, Budapest

423 *IT BEGINS WITH MARRIAGE*, János Vaszary; two drawings for settings, 1932; Belvarosi Theatre, Budapest
  Nos. 421–423 lent by the Artist

OLÁH, Gustave   BUDAPEST

424–425 *MINUTE OPERA*, Darius Milhaud; two drawings for settings
  Lent by Charles Rosner, Budapest

ITALY

de CHIRICO, Giorgio   FLORENCE

426 *LA JARRE*, Swedish Ballet, Rolf de Maré, producer, Paris, 1924; drawing for setting

Lent by Les Archives Internationales de la Danse, Paris

For other Italian designers see section *Theatre Art of the Renaissance and Baroque Periods*

LATVIA

MUNCIS, Jan   RIGA

THE BLUE BIRD, Maeterlinck; drawing for setting, National Theatre, Riga, 1933:

427 —The Kingdom of the Future

PEER GYNT, Ibsen; drawing for setting, National Theatre, Riga, 1933:

428 —In the Mountains
  Nos. 427 to 428 lent by the Artist

SWEDEN

ÅHRÉN, Uno   STOCKHOLM

STRANGE INTERLUDE, O'Neill; two drawings for settings, Royal Dramatic Theatre, Stockholm:

429 —Act VII

430 —Act IX
  Lent by the Royal Dramatic Theatre, Stockholm

GRÜNEWALD, Isaac   STOCKHOLM

FIESCO, Schiller; eleven costume drawings, Royal Dramatic Theatre, Stockholm:

431 —Asserato

*432 —Bourgognino

433 —Bourgognino

434 —Calcagno

*435 —Dorio

436 —Leonora

437 —Lomellino

438 —Male character

439 —Male character

440 —Male character

441 —Female character

*442–448 *FIESCO*, Schiller; seven drawings for settings, Royal Dramatic Theatre, Stockholm

ANTONY AND CLEOPATRA, Shakespeare; ten costume drawings, Royal Dramatic Theatre, Stockholm:

449 —Antony
450 —Caesar
451 —Enobarbus, Philo, and Demetrius
452 —Dolabella and Proculeius
453 —Pompeius
454 —Proculeius
455 —Charmian
456 —Mariner
457 —Iras
458 —Servant of Cleopatra

459 —CAVALLERIA RUSTICANA, Mascagni; drawing for setting, Royal Dramatic Theatre, Stockholm

460-461 SAMSON AND DELILAH, Saint-Saëns; two drawings for settings, Royal Dramatic Theatre, Stockholm

462-464 SAKUNTALA, Reyer; three drawings for settings, Royal Dramatic Theatre, Stockholm

Nos. 431 to 464 lent by the Royal Dramatic Theatre, Stockholm

MOLANDER, Olov and
SKAWONIUS Sven-Erik   STOCKHOLM

465-467 GREEN PASTURES, Marc Connelly; three drawings for Frieze of Promenade, Royal Dramatic Theatre, Stockholm

468 GREEN PASTURES Marc Connelly; model for setting, Royal Dramatic Theatre, Stockholm

*469-471 MASTER OLOF, August Strindberg; three drawings for settings, Royal Dramatic Theatre, Stockholm

Nos. 465 to 471 lent by the Royal Dramatic Theatre, Stockholm

SJÖBERG, Alf   STOCKHOLM

472 THE HOLY FAMILY, Rudolf Varnlund; drawing for setting; Royal Dramatic Theatre, Stockholm

Lent by the Royal Dramatic Theatre, Stockholm

SKÖLD, Otte   STOCKHOLM

473-474 MEDEA, Euripides; two drawings for settings, Royal Dramatic Theatre, Stockholm

MEDEA, Euripides; six costume drawings, Royal Dramatic Theatre, Stockholm:

475 —Jason
476 —Jason's Escort
477 —Aegeus' Escort
478 —Chorus
479 —Chorus
480 —Chorus

THE FAITHFUL, John Masefield; two drawings for settings, Royal Dramatic Theatre, Stockholm:

481 —Inside Kira's Palace
482 —Concert House

Nos. 473 to 482 lent by the Royal Dramatic Theatre, Stockholm

SWITZERLAND

APPIA, Adolphe: see section *Pioneers of the Modern Theatre Art*, page 46

UNITED STATES OF AMERICA

BERNSTEIN, Aline   NEW YORK
483 THE PORCELAIN PALACE, scenario from Hans Anderson's story "The Nightingale;" model of setting, 1933

*484-488 THE PORCELAIN PALACE, scenario from Hans Anderson's story "The Nightingale;" five costume drawings, 1933

Nos. 483 to 488 lent by the Artist

BRAGDON, Claude　　　　　NEW YORK

*489 *THE GLITTERING GATE*, Lord Dun-
　　sany; drawing for setting, 1933

　　THE GODS OF THE MOUNTAIN,
　　Lord Dunsany; two drawings for set-
　　tings, 1933:
490 —Scene 1
491 —Scene 2
　　　　　　Nos. 489 to 491 lent by the Artist

DREYFUSS, Henry　　　　　NEW YORK

492 *SALOME*, Oscar Wilde; one large and six
　　small drawings for settings, 1933
　　　　　　　　　　　Lent by the Artist

ENTERS, Angna　　　　　NEW YORK

493 *SPANISH MEDIEVAL NIGHT'S
　　DREAM*; drawing for setting, based on
　　the courtyard of the ruined palace of
　　Charles V in the Alhambra, 1933

494 *SPANISH MEDIEVAL NIGHT'S
　　DREAM*; six costume drawings, 1933:
　　Medieval Night's Dream, Auto da Fé,
　　Pavana, Inquisition Virgin, Boy Cardi-
　　nal, Santa España del Cruz

495 *BALLET MACABRE*; three figure draw-
　　ings based on artists' implements and
　　model forms, 1933

*496 *DIONYSIAN GREECE IN NEW
　　YORK*; drawing for setting with fig-
　　ures, 1932

497 *PAGAN GREECE*; costume drawing for
　　Artemis, 1933

498 *THE HOLY VIRGIN PURSUED BY
　　SATAN*; costume drawing, 1933

499 *ODALISQUE*; costume drawing, 1933
　　　　Nos. 493 to 499 lent by the Ehrich Galleries,
　　　　　　　　　　　　　　　　New York

ESSMAN, Manuel　　　　　NEW YORK

500 *TWILIGHT IMPERIALISM*, Robert
　　Medloe; drawing for setting with plas-
　　tic stage, 1933

*501-502 *THE TOWER*, Herbert Biberman;
　　two drawings for settings, 1933: Setting
　　for a stage of mobile forms with simul-
　　taneous action on various levels

503 *RAZZ MANHATTAN*, Martin Eyre;
　　drawing for Neo-Actualist setting with
　　electric transcription broadcast of an
　　historic event used as sound background,
　　1933
　　　　　　Nos. 500 to 503 lent by the Artist

GEDDES, Norman Bel　　　　NEW YORK

　　KING LEAR, Shakespeare; five drawings
　　of settings, 1917:
504 —Courtyard of Gloucester's Castle, pre-
　　liminary study
*505 —Courtyard of Gloucester's Castle
*506 —The Throne of Lear
507 —Between the Camps
508 —Hut on the Heath

　　KING LEAR, Shakespeare; two costume
　　drawings, 1917:
509 —Duke of Albany
510 —Duke of Cornwall

　　DIVINE COMEDY, Dante; four draw-
　　ings for settings, 1920:
511 —The Earth Opens
512 —Inferno
513 —The Gates of Purgatory
514 —Paradise

515-518 *DIVINE COMEDY*, Dante; four
　　plaster masks, 1920

519 *DIVINE COMEDY*, Dante; photograph
　　of settings showing stage structure, 1920

520 *LAZARUS LAUGHED*, Eugene O'Neill;
　　model of setting, 1927

521 *LAZARUS LAUGHED*, Eugene O'Neill;
　　five photographs of model of setting,
　　1927

522-523 *LAZARUS LAUGHED*, Eugene
　　O'Neill; two costume drawings, 1927

524-533 LAZARUS LAUGHED, Eugene O'Neill; forty drawings for masks, 1927

AIDA, Verdi; four drawings for settings, 1933:
534 —Act I
535 —Act II
536 —Act III
537 —Act IV

538-540 AIDA, Verdi; three costume drawings, 1933

AIDA, Verdi; four paper models for settings, 1933:
541 —Act I
542 —Act II
543 —Act III
544 —Act IV

545 AIDA, Verdi; wooden model for setting, 1933: Act III

546 KING LEAR, Shakespeare; wooden model for setting, 1933: The Throne of Lear
Nos. 504 to 546 lent by the Artist

GORELIK, Mordecai   NEW YORK
THEY SHALL NOT DIE, John Wexley; two drawings for settings, 1933:
547 —Act I, Jail in Scottsville, Alabama
548 —Act II, Courtroom, Dexter, Alabama

PROCESSIONAL, John Howard Lawson; two drawings for settings, 1924:
549 —Act I, On the Fourth of July
550 —Act II, The Labor Temple
Nos. 547 to 550 lent by the Artist

JONES, Robert Edmond
          HOLLYWOOD, CALIFORNIA
551 RICHARD III, Shakespeare; drawing for setting, 1920
Lent by Miss Fania Mindell, New York

552 RICHARD III, Shakespeare; drawing for setting, 1920: The Wooing of Lady Anne

Lent by the Artist

MACBETH, Shakespeare; four drawings for settings, 1921:
*553 —The Letter Scene
Lent by Sidney Howard, New York

554 —The Sleep-walking Scene
555 —The Three Witches
556 —Banquo's Ghost
Lent by Dr. Smith Ely Jelliffe, New York

557 SWORDS, Sidney Howard; drawing for setting, 1922
Lent by Sidney Howard, New York

558 HAMLET, Shakespeare; drawing for setting, 1923
Lent by Mrs. E. C. MacVeagh, New York

559 HAMLET, Shakespeare; drawing for setting, 1933: The Madness of Ophelia
Lent by Lee Simonson, New York

560 DESIRE UNDER THE ELMS, Eugene O'Neill; drawing for setting, 1924
Lent by Walter Huston, Beverly Hills, Cal.

561 SALVATION, Sidney Howard; drawing for setting, 1928
Lent by Sidney Howard, New York

562 THE GREEN PASTURES, Marc Connelly; drawing for setting, 1929: The Prayer of Moses

563 LA GIOCONDA, d'Annunzio; drawing for setting: Act III, The Sculptor's Studio
Nos. 562 to 563 lent by Mrs. Frances G. Wickes, New York

564 CAMILLE, Dumas; drawing for setting, 1932; Act V, Marguerite's Bedroom
Lent by Miss Lillian Gish, New York

OTHELLO, Shakespeare; three drawings for settings, 1933:
*565 —A Street in Venice
566 —The Council Chamber
567 —Desdemona's Bedchamber

568 OTHELLO, Shakespeare; costume drawing, 1933: Desdemona
Nos. 565 to 568 lent by the Artist

JORGULESCO, Jonel   NEW YORK

THE TEMPEST, Shakespeare; three drawings for settings, 1933:

569 —Prologue
570 —Act II, Scene 2
571 —Epilogue

Lent by the Artist

KARSON, Nat   NEW YORK

THE OPERA RACKET, Walter Schmidt; three drawings for settings, 1933:

572 —Dungeon Scene
573 —Racketeer's Jail Cell
574 —Mussolini's Office

THE COLOR BOX, Ben Oakland and Milton Drake; three drawings for settings, 1933:

575 —Act I, finale, The Red Dawn, first movement
*576 —Act I, finale, The Red Dawn, second movement
577 —Dance Setting

Nos. 572 to 577 lent by the Artist

LAUTERER, Arch   BENNINGTON, VERMONT

THE VIKINGS AT HELGELAND, Ibsen; four drawings for settings, 1933:

578 —Act I, A Sheltered Place
579 —Act II, Gunner's Feast Hall
580 —Act III, The Dais in Gunner's Hall
581 —Act IV, The Burial Place

*582 THE VIKINGS AT HELGELAND, Ibsen; model for setting, 1933

Nos. 578 to 582 lent by the Artist

MIELZINER, Jo   NEW YORK

THE YELLOW JACK, Sidney Howard; three drawings for settings, 1933:

583 —Field Laboratory, East Africa
*584 —Fever Victims, Cuba, 1900
585 —A Laboratory, London

THE RED GENERAL, Hermann Ungar; five drawings for settings, 1930:

586 —Waiting Room

587 —Side Street, Petrograd
588 —Meeting in Winter Palace
589 —Scene 4
590 —War Zone

Nos. 583 to 590 lent by the Artist

OENSLAGER, Donald M.   NEW YORK

HAMLET, Shakespeare; five drawings for settings, 1933:

591 —Act I, Scene 1, Platform before the Castle
592 —Act III, Scene 2, Hall in the Castle
*593 —Act III, Scene 4, The Queen's Closet
594 —Act V, Scene 1, A Churchyard
595 —Act V, Scene 2, Another Hall in the Castle

596-597 THE BIRDS, Aristophanes; two drawings for settings for a modern version done as a satire on aviation, 1927

THE FLYING DUTCHMAN, Wagner; two drawings for settings, 1930:

598 —Act I
599 —Act II

THE EMPEROR JONES, Eugene O'Neill; two drawings for settings, 1931:

600 —Before the Voodoo Altar
601 —Convict Scene

602 CASINA, Plautus; drawing for setting, 1932

Nos. 591 to 602 lent by the Artist

PETERS, Rollo   NEW YORK

603 STEPHEN FOSTER, Mary Ward and Arthur Henry; drawing for setting, 1933

604-605 STEPHEN FOSTER, Mary Ward and Arthur Henry; two costume drawings, 1933

Nos. 603 to 605 lent by the Artist

REYNOLDS, James   NEW YORK

606 ATHENA PROTECTRESS, drawing for setting, 1933

ATHENA PROTECTRESS, two drawings for costumes, 1933:

607 —Headdress for Samian Patrician, 300 B. C.—man

608 —Headdress for Samian Patrician, 300 B. C.—woman

Nos. 606 to 608 lent by the artist

SIMONSON, Lee   NEW YORK

 HAMLET, Shakespeare; three drawings for settings, 1933:

609 —Prelude

*610 —Act I, Scene 4

611 —Act V, Scene 1

Lent by the Artist

THOMPSON, Woodman   NEW YORK

612–613 *IPHIGENIA IN TAURIS*, Euripides; two drawings for settings, 1933

614–616 *IPHIGENIA IN TAURIS*, Euripi-

des; three costume drawings, 1933

Nos. 612 to 616 lent by the Artist

THROCKMORTON, Cleon   NEW YORK

 THE EMPEROR JONES, Eugene O'Neill; four drawings for settings, 1933:

617 —The Edge of the Woods

618 —Convict Scene

619 —Hold of the Slave Ship

620 —At the Foot of a Great Tree

*621 *THE EMPEROR JONES*, Eugene O'Neill; model of setting, 1933

Nos. 617 to 621 lent by the Artist

WENGER, John   New York

 THE AWAKENING, Vera Gordova; four drawings for settings, 1933:

622 —Act I, Scene 1, Outside the Pagoda

623 —Act II, Scene 1, A Balcony

624 —Act II, Scene 2, A Salon

625 —Act III, Scene 2, Apotheosis

Lent by the Artist

UNION OF SOCIALIST SOVIET REPUBLICS

PRE-REVOLUTIONARY PERIOD

The later work of Russian expatriates, Bakst, Gontcharova, Larionoff, Survage, is listed under France and the School of Paris. The U. S. S. R. exhibit arrived three weeks late so that it could not be cataloged with the material at hand. For this reason, also, the illustrated items bear no asterisks. Many corrections and additional information have been provided by Prof. H. W. L. Dana, Cambridge, Massachusetts.

DOBUZHINSKY, Mstislaff   Moscow

626–629 *SORROWS OF THE SPIRIT (GORE OT UMA)*, Griboiedoff; four drawings for settings, Moscow Art Theatre, 1906

Lent by M. Brodsky, Leningrad

GOLOVINE, Alexander   Moscow

 BORIS GODUNOFF, Moussorgsky; drawing for setting, 1908:

630 —Scene in the Kremlin

 MASKED BALL, Lermontoff; two drawings for settings, 1917:

631 —House of Joy

632 —Last Scene

 THE STORM, Ostrovsky; drawing for setting, 1912–1913:

633 —Interior

Nos. 630 to 633 lent by Bakrushin Theatre Museum, Moscow

SOUDEKINE, Sergei   PARIS

 TALES OF HOFFMAN, Offenbach; two drawings for settings, 1909:

634 —Scene with the Dolls

635 —Scene in Venice

Lent by Bakrushin Theatre Museum, Moscow

AKIMOFF, Nicolai — LENINGRAD

636 *THE WIFE*, Troneff; model for setting, State Dramatic Theatre, Leningrad, 1926

637 *ARMORED TRAIN* 14.69, V. Ivanoff; model for setting, State Dramatic Theatre, Leningrad, 1927

Nos. 636 to 637 lent by the Museum of the State Dramatic Theatre, Leningrad

638–651 *ROBESPIERRE*, F. F. Raskolnikoff; fourteen drawings, State Theatre, Leningrad, 1931

652 *LA BELLE HÉLÈNE*, Offenbach; drawing, Little Opera, Leningrad, 1932

653 *THE JUDGMENT*, V. Kirshon; drawing, State Theatre(?), Leningrad, 1932

654–655 *FEAR (STRAKH)*, Afinogenoff; two drawings, State Theatre(?), Leningrad, 1933

HAMLET, Shakespeare; four drawings for costumes, Vakhtangoff Theatre, Moscow, 1933:

656 —Hamlet

657 —Hamlet

658 —Polonius

659 —Countryman

HAMLET, Shakespeare; two drawings for settings, Vakhtangoff Theatre, Moscow, 1933:

660 —House of Polonius

661 —Act II

BORIS GODUNOFF, Moussorgsky; drawing for setting, not yet produced, 1933:

662 —The Inn

Nos. 638 to 662 lent by the Artist

CHUPIATCH — LENINGRAD

663 *THE LUCRATIVE POSITION*, Ostrovsky; model for setting, State Dramatic Theatre, Leningrad, 1933

Lent by the Museum of the State Dramatic Theatre, Leningrad

DMITRIEFF, A. I. — LENINGRAD

664 *THE MEISTERSINGERS*, Wagner; drawing, Opera, Leningrad

Lent by the Opera Museum, Leningrad

DMITRIEFF, A. I.: See also VYESNINE

KODOSEVITCH, Valentin — Leningrad

665–668 —*OTHELLO*, Shakespeare; four drawings

Lent by the Artist

KRUMMER — LENINGRAD

669 *THE BATH*, Mayakovsky; model for settings, State Dramatic Theatre, Leningrad, 1930

Lent by the Museum of the State Dramatic Theatre, Leningrad

KUSHNER — LENINGRAD

670 *THE FLEA*, Mayakovsky; model for setting, State Dramatic Theatre, Leningrad, 1928

Lent by the Museum of the State Dramatic Theatre, Leningrad

LEBEDEFF — LENINGRAD

671 *THE JEST*, Sem Benelli; model for setting, State Dramatic Theatre, Leningrad, 1923

Lent by the Museum of the State Dramatic Theatre, Leningrad

LEVINE, Moisei — LENINGRAD

672–675 *WOZZEK*, Alban Berg; four drawings for costumes, 1927

Seven drawings for costumes, Little Opera, Leningrad, 1932:

676 —Merchant

677 —Boyar

678 —Armed Boyar

679 —Tsar

680 —Tsarina

681 —Peasant

682 —Peasant

683 *THE FAIR AT SOROCHINSK*, Moussorgsky; drawing for setting

THE FAIR AT SOROCHINSK, Moussorgsky; two drawings for costumes:

684 —Woman
685 —Woman

686 *THE FRUITS OF EDUCATION*, L. N. Tolstoi; eight drawings for costumes
Nos. 672 to 686 lent by the Artist

687-689 *KAMARINSKY MUZHIK;* three drawings for settings, Little Opera, Leningrad, 1933
Lent by the Little Opera Museum, Leningrad

690 *ALL QUIET ON THE WESTERN FRONT*, Remarque; model for setting, State Dramatic Theatre, Leningrad, 1932

691 *JOY STREET*, Zarchi; model for setting, State Dramatic Theatre, Leningrad, 1932
Nos. 690 to 691 lent by the Museum of the State Dramatic Theatre, Leningrad

LUTZE, V. V.   LENINGRAD
692 *BREAD*, V. Kirshon; model for setting, State Dramatic Theatre, Leningrad, 1930
Lent by the Museum of the State Dramatic Theatre, Leningrad

MEDUNETSKY: See STENBERG
MEYERHOLD(?)   Moscow
693 *MANDATE*, Nicolai Erdman; model for setting, Meyerhold Theatre, Moscow, 1925; K. A. Soste, technician
Lent by the Bakrushin Theatre Museum, Moscow

NIVINSKY, I.   Moscow
PRINCESS TURANDOT, Carlo Gozzi (1722-1806), music by I. Sizoff; Third Studio of the Moscow Art Theatre (Vakhtangoff), Moscow, 1921; three color-lithographs from the book *Printsessa Turandot*, Moscow, 1922:

694 —Setting for Scene III
695 —Setting for Scene VI
696 —Costume for the Caliph
Books lent by Mrs. Richard C. Wood, Lee Simonson, Alfred H. Barr, Jr.

SCHLEPIANOFF   Moscow
697 *POEM OF THE AX*, N. Pogodin; model for setting, Theatre of the Revolution, Moscow, 1931
Lent by the Museum of the Theatre of the Revolution, Moscow

SHESTAKOFF   Moscow
698 *ECHO*, Bill-Belotserkovski; model for setting, Theatre of the Revolution, Moscow, 1924

699 *SORROWS OF THE SPIRIT (GORE OT UMA)*, Griboiedoff; model for setting, Meyerhold Theatre, Moscow, 1928. Meyerhold changed the title to *Sorrow to the Spirit (Gore Umu)*.
Nos. 698 to 699 lent by the Bakrushin Theatre Museum, Moscow

STENBERG   Moscow
700 *ALL GOD'S CHILLUN (NEGR)*, Eugene O'Neill; model for setting. Kamerny (Tairoff) Theatre, Moscow, 1929
Lent by the Museum of the Kamerny Theatre, Moscow

STENBERG and MEDUNETSKY   Moscow
701 *THE STORM*, Ostrovsky; model for setting, Kamerny (Tairoff) Theatre, Moscow, 1923-1924
Lent by the Bakrushin Theatre Museum, Moscow

VYESNINE, Alexander(?) or   Moscow
DMITRIEFF, A. I.(?)
SERFS, P. P. Gnedich; two drawings for settings, Little Theatre, Moscow, 1921.
702 —Blue Interior
703 —Gold Interior
Lent by the Museum of the Little Theatre, Moscow

UNKNOWN LENINGRAD

704 *UNCLE TOM'S CABIN*, after Harriet Beecher Stowe; model for setting, Theatre of the Young Audience (Children's Theatre), Leningrad(?)

Lent by the Museum of the Theatre of the Young Spectator, Leningrad (?)

UNKNOWN LENINGRAD

705 *TOM SAWYER*, after Mark Twain; Theatre of the Young Audience (Children's Theatre), Leningrad(?)

Lent by the Museum of the Theatre of the Young Spectator, Leningrad(?)

UNKNOWN MOSCOW

706 *THE RAILS ARE HUMMING*, V. Kirshon; model for setting, Moscow Trade Union Theatre (M. O. S. P. S., formerly M. G. S. P. S.), Moscow, 1929

Lent by the Bakrushin Theatre Museum, Moscow

UNKNOWN MOSCOW

707 *THE UNKNOWN SOLDIER*, Paul Raynal; model for setting, Kamerny (Tairoff) Theatre, Moscow

Lent by the Museum of the Kamerny Theatre, Moscow

GAMREKELI, Irakli   TIFLIS, GEORGIA

ANZOR, S. Shanshiashvili; drawing for setting, Roustaveli Theatre, Tiflis, 1928, producer, Sandro Akmeteli

708—Act III, Caucasian Village

*709 THE BUSINESS MAN; drawing for setting, Roustaveli Theatre, Tiflis, 1928, producer, Sandro Akmeteli

LAMARA; drawing for setting, Roustaveli Theatre, Tiflis, 1929, producer, Sandro Akmeteli

710 —Act IV

*711 TETNOULD, S. Dadiani; drawing for setting, Roustaveli Theatre, Tiflis, 1932, producer, Sandro Akmeteli

THE ROBBERS, Schiller; three drawings for settings, Roustaveli Theatre, Tiflis, 1933, producer, Sandro Akmeteli

712 —Act II, Scene 2, Bohemian Forest
713 —Scene 2, The Inn
714 —Setting

Nos. 708 to 714 lent by the Roustaveli Theatre Museum, Tiflis

LUTZE, V. V.   LENINGRAD

715 ALL QUIET ON THE WESTERN FRONT, M. Zagorsky, after Remarque; model for setting, State Dramatic Theatre, Leningrad, 1932, director, V. V. Lutze

Lent by the Museum of the State Dramatic Theatre, Leningrad

NADAREISHVILI, S.   TIFLIS, GEORGIA

716 ABESALOM AND EUTERP; drawing for four settings, Roustaveli Theatre, Tiflis

717 ABESALOM AND EUTERP; drawing for two costumes, Roustaveli Theatre, Tiflis

Nos. 716, 717 lent by the Roustaveli Theatre Museum, Tiflis

NIVINSKY, I.   Moscow

*718–721 PRINCESS TURANDOT, Carlo Gozzi (1722–1806), music by I. Sizoff; four drawings for settings, Third Studio of the Moscow Art Theatre (Vakhtangoff), Moscow, 1921

Lent by Mme. Vakhtangoff, Moscow

PRINCESS TURANDOT; five drawings for costumes, 1921

*722 —Tartalia
*723 —Brighella
724 —Pantalone
725 —Truffaldino
726 —Costume

Lent by Mme. Vakhtangoff, Moscow

OTZHELI, P.   TIFLIS, GEORGIA

727–728 URIEL ACOSTA, Gutzkoff; two drawings for settings, Roustaveli Theatre, Tiflis, producer, K. Mardjanoff

Lent by the Roustaveli Theatre Museum, Tiflis

RINDIN, V.   Moscow

*729 THE UNKNOWN SOLDIERS, Leonid Pervomaiski; model for setting, Kamerny Theatre, Moscow, 1932, producer, A. Tairoff

THE UNKNOWN SOLDIERS, Leonid Pervomaiski; two drawings for costumes, Kamerny Theatre, Moscow, 1932, producer, A. Tairoff

730 —Soldier
731 —Man in evening clothes

Nos. 729 to 731 lent by the Museum of the Kamerny Theatre, Moscow

732 *WE ARE STRENGTH;* model for setting, Moscow Children's Theatre, producer, E. Mei

WE ARE STRENGTH; two drawings for costumes, Moscow Children's Theatre, producer, E. Mei

733 —White Children

734 —Yellow Children

Nos. 732 to 734 lent by the Children's Theatre, Museum, Moscow

STENBERG, W. and G.   Moscow

*735-736 *ALL GOD'S CHILLUN GOT WINGS (Negr),* Eugene O'Neill; two drawings for costumes, Kamerny Theatre, Moscow, 1929, producer, A. Tairoff

Lent by the Museum of the Kamerny Theatre, Moscow

VARPEKH, M.   Moscow

737-739 *WE WILL SETTLE IT BETWEEN OURSELVES,* Ostrovsky; three drawings for settings, Theatre of the Young Spectator, Moscow, director, V. Kolesaieff

740-741 *WE WILL SETTLE IT BETWEEN OURSELVES,* Ostrovsky; two drawings for costumes, Theatre of the Young Spectator, Moscow, director, V. Kolesaieff

742-743 *GUARD OF HIMSELF,* Calderón; two drawings for costumes, Theatre of the Young Spectator, Moscow, director, L. Volkoff

Nos. 737 to 743 lent by the Museum of the Theatre of the Young Spectator, Moscow

VOLKOFF, B. U.   Moscow

744 *THE RAILS ARE HUMMING,* V. Kirshon; drawing for setting, Moscow Trade Union Theatre (M.O.S.P.S., formerly M.G.S.P.S.), Moscow, 1929

THE REVOLT, Furmanoff; drawing for setting, Moscow Trade Union Theatre (M. O. S. P. S., formerly M. G. S. P. S.), Moscow, 1927

745 —The Market

THE MOB, Shapovalenko; drawing for setting, Moscow Trade Union Theatre (M. O. S. P. S., formerly M. G. S. P. S.), Moscow, 1926

746 —The Bridge

Nos. 744 to 746 lent by the Bakrushin Theatre Museum, Moscow

UNKNOWN

747 *MARRIAGE,* Gogol; model for setting

748 *CHERNI YAR;* model for setting

CORRECTIONS IN THE SOVIET SECTION

653 *For* State Theatre (?), Leningrad, 1932 *read* State Dramatic Theatre, Leningrad, 1933

662 *For* not yet produced, 1933 *read* 1927, Leningrad Opera

664 *For* drawing, Opera *read* four drawings for settings, Little Opera

684 *For* two drawings for costumes *read* drawing for two costumes, Little Opera Theatre, Leningrad

700 *For* STENBERG *read* STENBERG, W. and G., *for* ALL GOD'S CHILLUN (NEGR) *read* ALL GOD'S CHILLUN GOT WINGS (NEGR)

706 *See* ADDITIONS TO THE SOVIET SECTION OF THE CATALOG, No. 744

707 *See* ADDITIONS TO THE SOVIET SECTION OF THE CATALOG, No. 729

OMISSIONS IN THE SOVIET SECTION

The following items were not sent by the U. S. S. R. 626-636, 638-651, 654-661, 663, 665-683, 685-690, 693, 694-699, 701-704, 705

PLATES

9 PRIMATICCIO

708.

10 PRIMATICCIO

17 RICCIUS SENENSIS   ORTENSIO

19 INIGO JONES

THE MASQUE OF QUEENS

20   INIGO JONES   *OBERON, THE FAERY PRINCE*

21 INIGO JONES   *OBERON, THE FAERY PRINCE*

23 INIGO JONES LUMINALIA

25 VIGARANI

Cielo aperto a filtro in fra

43 IUVARA

48 BIBIENA

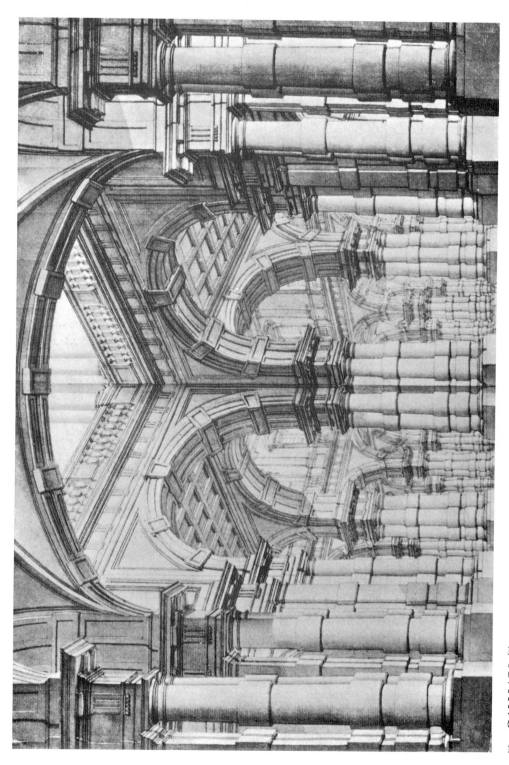

53 GALLIARI (?)

HERMANNSCHLACHT

städt. Theatermuseum
Meiningen *5YL*

95 SAXE-MEININGEN

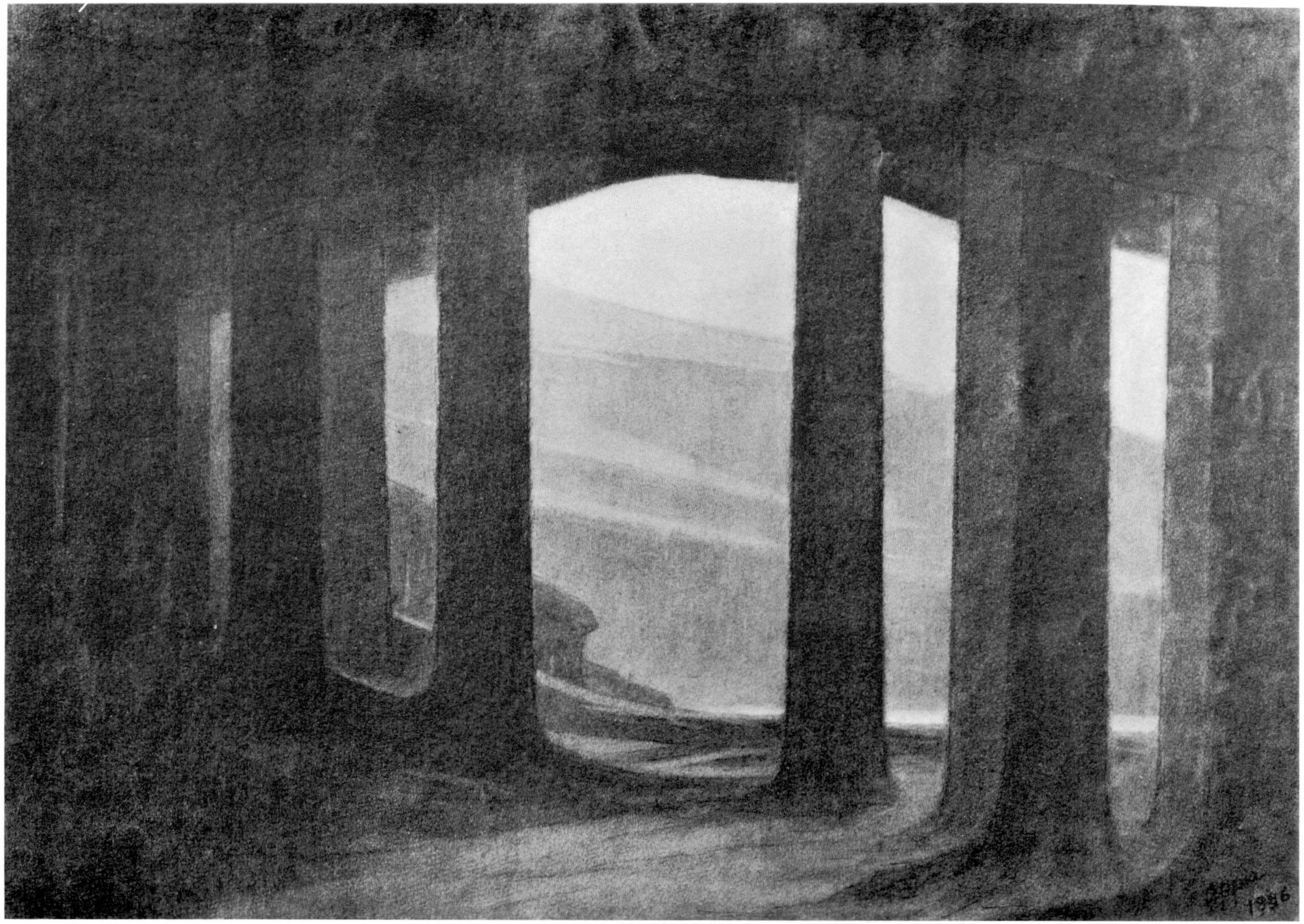

105 APPIA *PARSIFAL*

THE RHEINGOLD

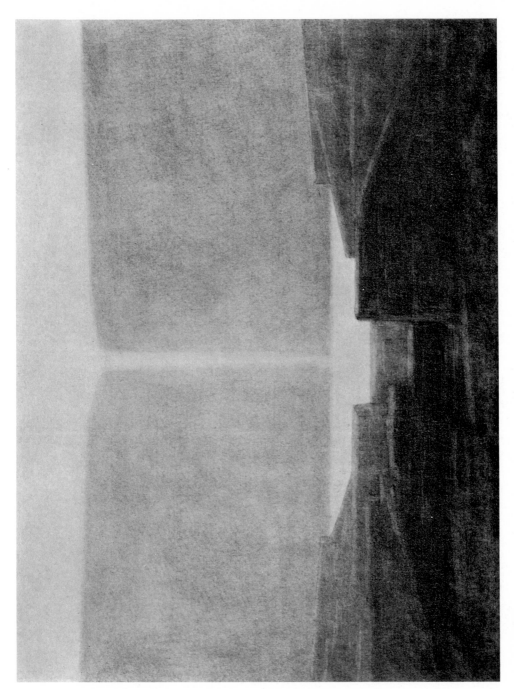

110 APPIA

123 CRAIG

134 CRAIG

145 STRNAD

KING LEAR

DANTON'S DEATH

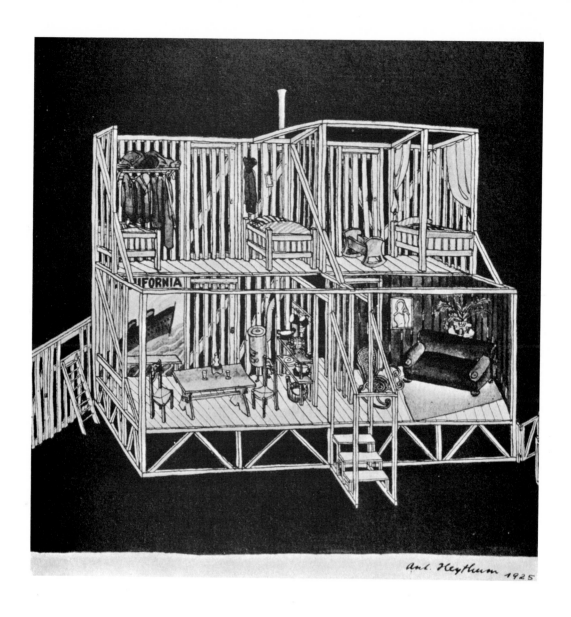

169 HEYTHUM

DESIRE UNDER THE ELMS

MERCHANT OF VENICE

THE GREAT GOD BROWN

THE GREAT GOD BROWN

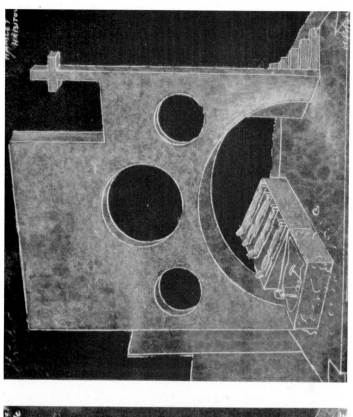

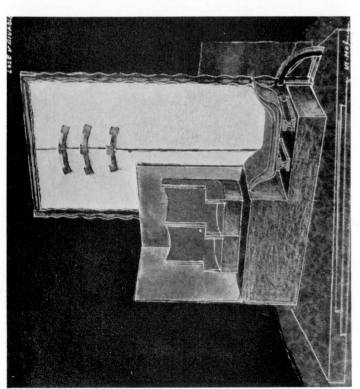

193   HOFMAN

R. U. R.

209 BLANCH

THE MERCHANT OF VENICE

274 BARSACQ

VOLPONE

267 BAKST

LE MARTYRE DE SAINT-SÉBASTIEN (?)

297 GONTCHAROVA   *LITURGY*

309 PICASSO   *PARADE*

311 PICASSO   *CUADRO FLAMENCO*

le bougier

326 VAKALO

THE PEACE

„FAUST" I.TEIL,
STUDIE ZU EINER SIMULTANBÜHNE 1:50

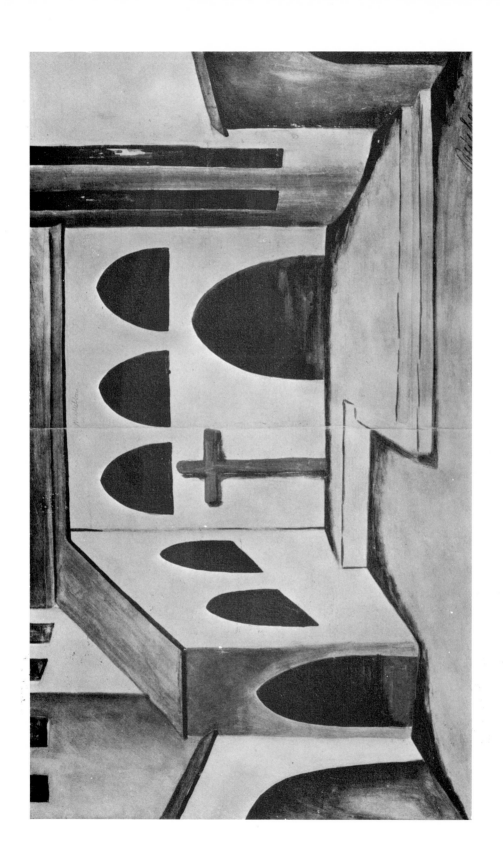

NACHFOLGE CHRISTI-SPIEL

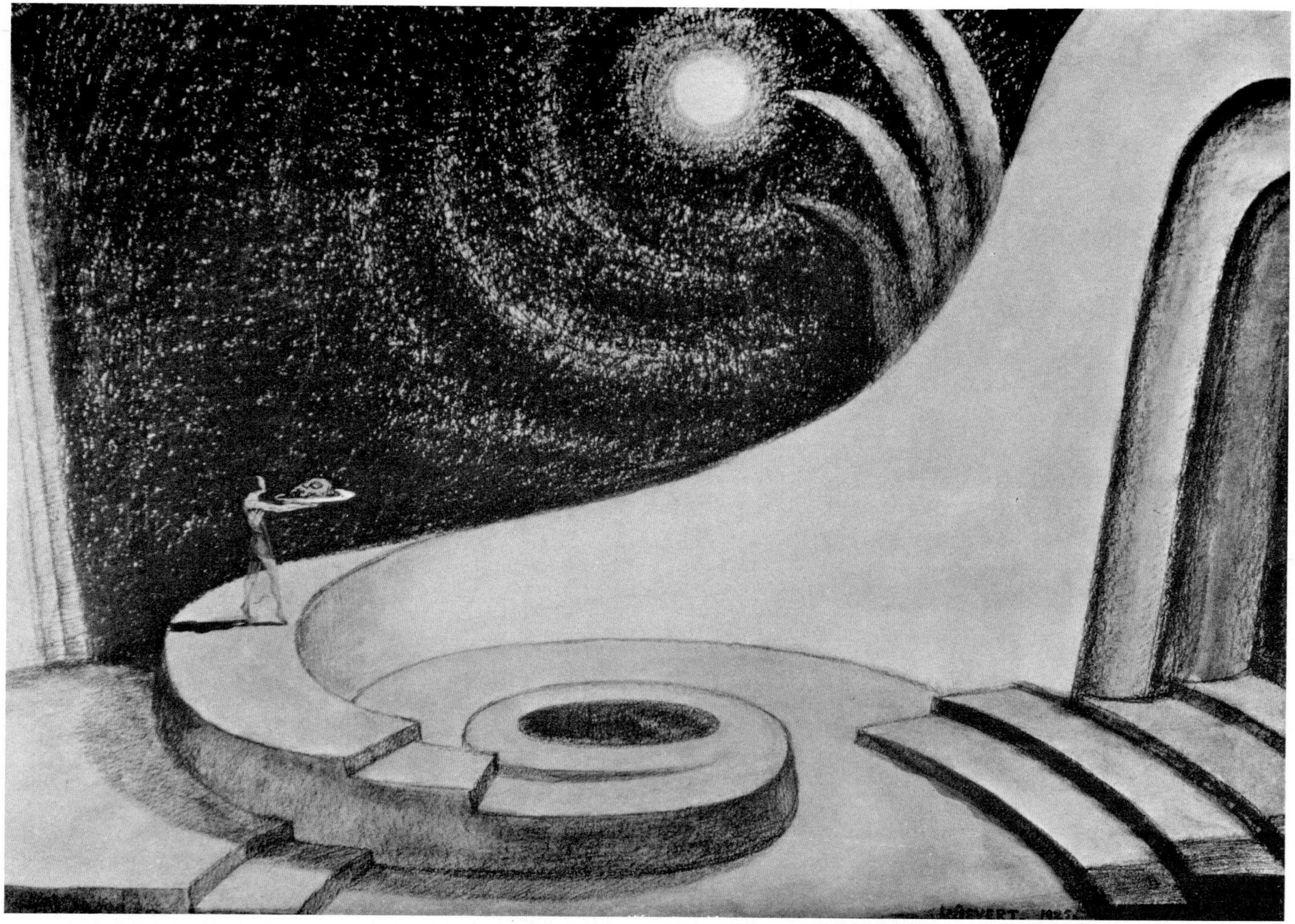

397 SIEVERT *SALOME*

432 GRÜNEWALD   *FIESCO*

435 GRÜNEWALD   *FIESCO*

FIESCO

469 MOLANDER AND SKAWONIUS   MASTER OLOF

484 BERNSTEIN

489 BRAGDON   *THE GLITTERING GATE*

A STAGE OF MOBILE FORMS

THE TOWER

501 ESSMAN

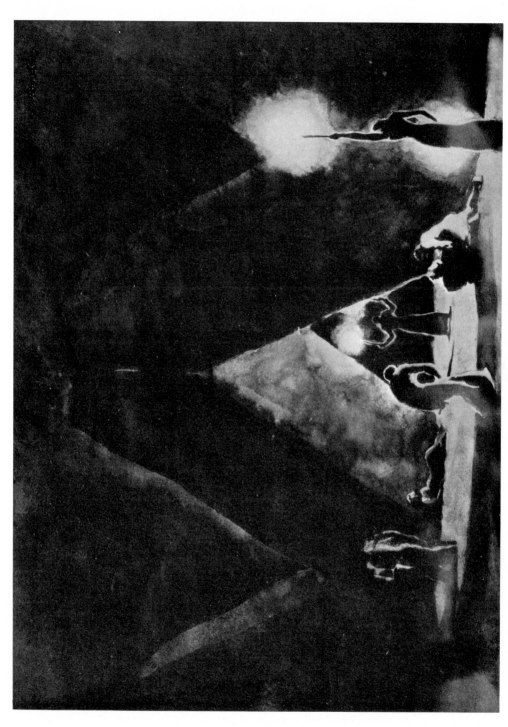

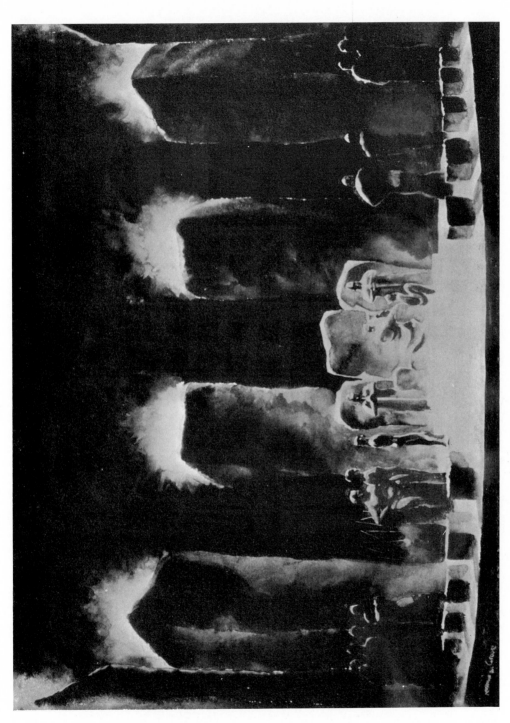

MACBETH

THE VIKINGS AT HELGELAND

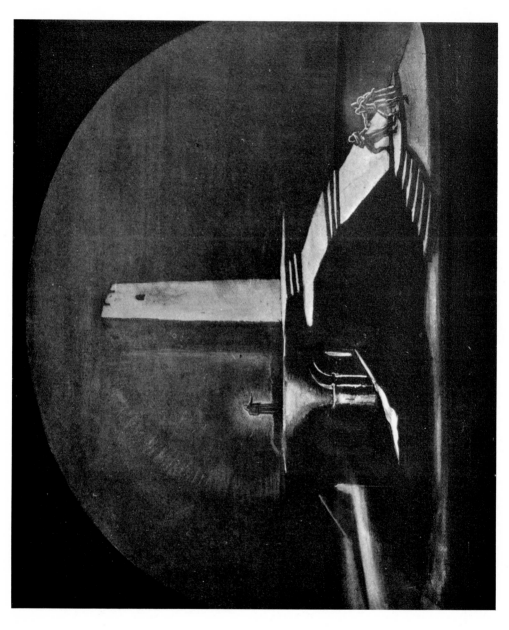

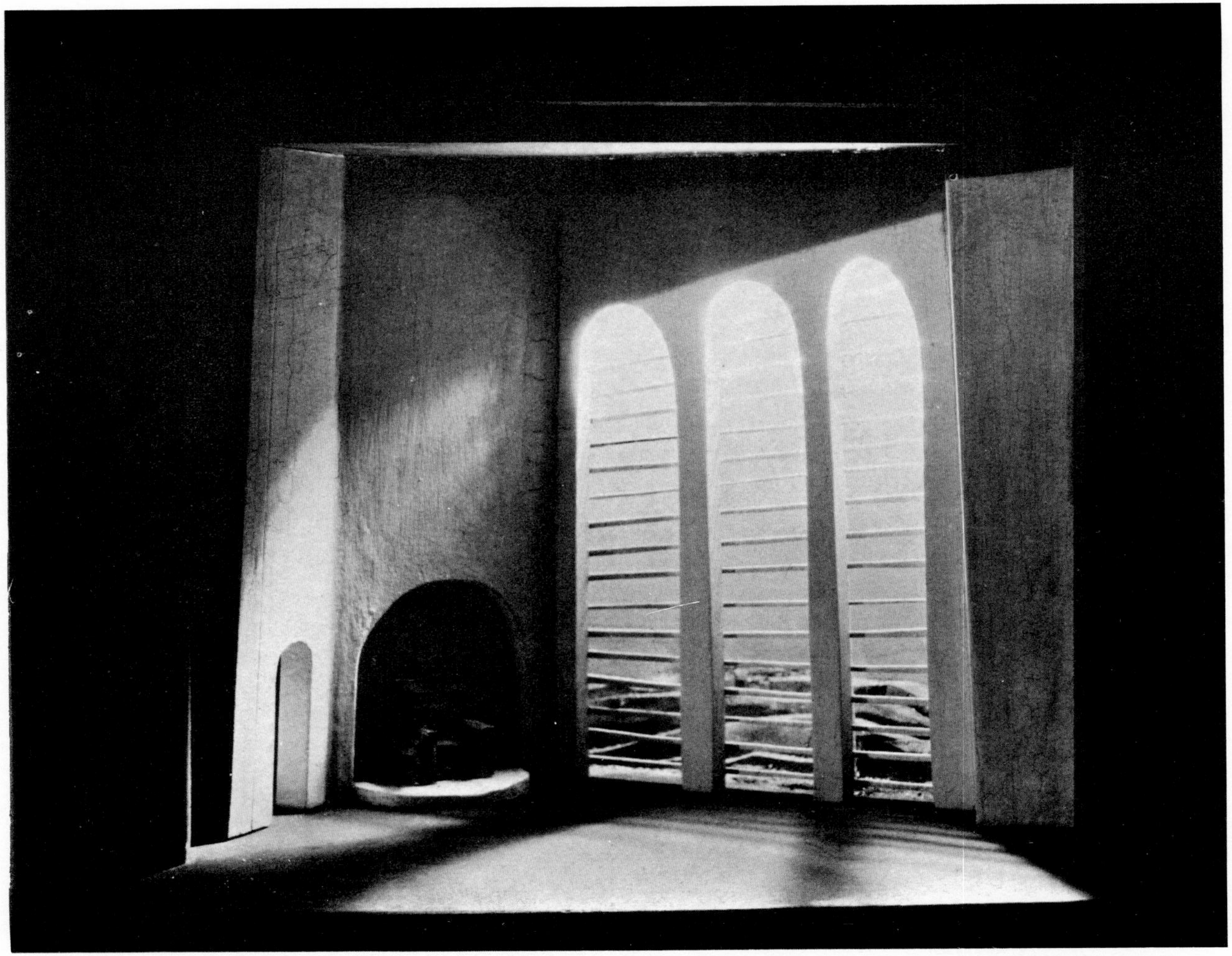

621 THROCKMORTON *THE EMPEROR JONES*

ARMORED TRAIN 14.69

(Double turntable—left, exterior; right, interior)

ALL GOD'S CHILLUN GOT WINGS

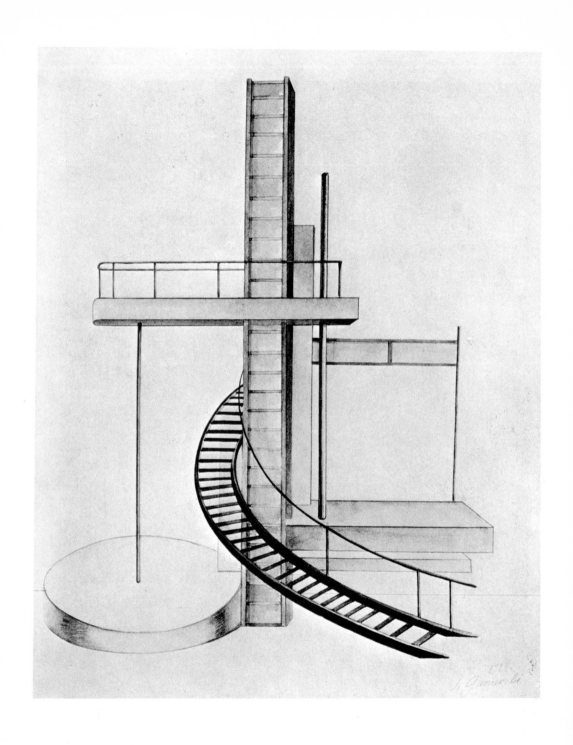

709 GAMREKELI

THE BUSINESS MAN

711   GAMREKELI   *TETNOULD*

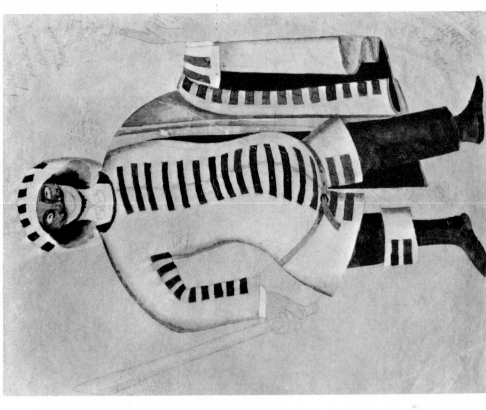

PRINCESS TURANDOT   723   NIVINSKY

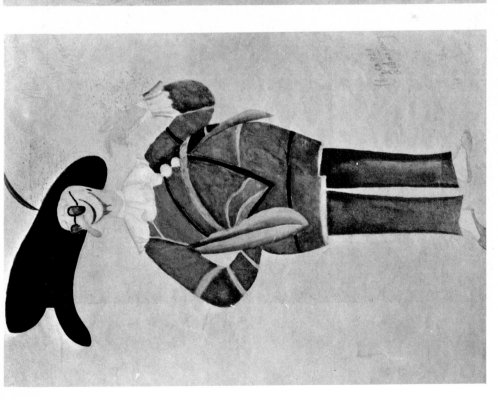

722   NIVINSKY   PRINCESS TURANDOT